CREATIVE
OUTDOOR
COOKING

Rose Cantrell

WEATHERVANE
BOOKS

contents

introduction

Today, almost everyone seems to be cooking outside—in the backyard, at a church picnic, or on a family camping vacation. With the multitude of outdoor grills and accessories on the market today, it is easy to cook in your own backyard or while traveling.

This book offers you a wide variety of ideas on how to get the most from a grill by cooking your entire meal, from appetizers to dessert, on the grill. A "Go-Along" chapter is included to give some creative ideas on accompaniments for an outdoor feast. During the summer months, while the sun is shining, why not discover the delights of cooking over glowing coals?

equipment

Outdoor grills come in four basic styles:

Brazier grill—This grill contains a fire bowl with a grid that fits directly over the fire bowl. Inexpensive models feature stationary grills that require you to cook all food at the same heat intensity. More expensive models have adjustable grids, allowing you to adjust the heat intensity as required by the food being prepared.

If you have a brazier grill with a stationary grid, the grid can be raised by filling four to six metal cans with pebbles and using these to support the grid.

Brazier grills equipped with half-hoods, rotisseries, and air dampers to control ventilation can also be purchased.

Hibachi—A small grill made popular by chefs in the Orient. It features an adjustable grid to control heat intensity, an air damper to control ventilation, and a coal rack to allow hot ashes to fall to the bottom. These grills are often placed directly on the table and the food is cooked as needed.

Kettle or covered grill—This grill offers versatility to outdoor cooking. It comes equipped with air dampers on the top and bottom to control ventilation, a coal rack near the bottom, and a grid in the middle of the grill.

Open, the kettle acts as a brazier; some models feature motorized rotisseries and skewers. With the lid down, the kettle acts as an oven. By adding a hickory chip and a pan of water, the kettle becomes a smoker.

Smoker—An outdoor slow cooker that utilizes coals for heat, hickory chips for flavor, and water to add moisture during the long cooking period. Most models feature dome lids for maximum heat utilization.

Before you use your grill, read the manufacturers instructions. Each grill has different features that you need to have knowledge of for your own safety and enjoyment.

starting the fire

Place the briquets (coals) in a pyramid in the center of the fire bowl. Soak them with lighting fluid. Let them stand 1 minute, then light. *Never use gasoline.* Allow coals to heat 30 minutes or until they turn gray before spreading them over the surface of the firebox.

Spread the charcoal layer slightly wider than the food to be cooked on the grill.

Place the grid over the coals and allow it to heat for a few minutes before adding food. (When cooking fish, it is wise to oil the grill lightly.)

Keep a bottle of water handy to extinguish any fires started by meat drippings.

cooking methods

Direct—Most outdoor cooking is done using this method. It is both fast and easy. The food is cooked by placing it on the grid directly above a bed of hot coals (usually 4 to 5 inches) and cooking for no longer than 30 minutes.

Indirect—This method is used to cook food in a covered kettle for long periods of time. This prevents the outside of the food from burning before the inside reaches the desired degree of doneness.

To use the indirect method, place an aluminum pan in the center of the firebox to catch the meat drippings. Pile hot coals around the pan. Cover the kettle. Adjust ventilation. Coals must be added every hour to keep the fire hot enough to cook the food.

Rotisserie or spit cooking—Although another method of indirect cooking, the coals are positioned differently from indirect cooking. Pile coals to the back of the firebox. Place drip pans under the meat on the spit to catch the drippings. Add coals every hour to keep the fire burning.

factors affecting cooking time

Intensity of heat—The amount of coals you use will affect the heat intensity. The more coals you use, the hotter the fire will be.

Temperature of food being cooked—It will take longer to cook refrigerated food than it will to cook room-temperature food.

Outside temperature—The lower the outside temperature, the longer it will take the food to cook.

Size of food being cooked—When arranging food on the grill, place larger pieces in the center of the grill, where the heat is more intense.

hamburger relish

Yield: ¾ cup

¼ **cup mayonnaise**
2 tablespoons prepared mustard
2 tablespoons tomato paste
½ **teaspoon sugar**
Dash of white pepper
**2 tablespoons finely chopped
      sweet pickles**
**2 tablespoons finely chopped
      Spanish onions**

Combine all ingredients; mix well. Refrigerate until ready for use.

devil's delight

This is for those who like a spicy-hot barbecue sauce.

Yield: ½ cup

2 tablespoons vegetable oil
1 teaspoon garlic juice
¼ **teaspoon cayenne pepper**
1 tablespoon Worcestershire sauce
2 tablespoons catsup
¼ **cup prepared mustard**

Mix ingredients in small saucepan. Heat on low heat until well-blended.

farm catsup

This recipe makes homemade catsup a lazy-man's job. By cooking it on your grill by the indirect method (see Index) or in a slow cooker, you need not monitor the kettle to keep it from scorching.

Yield: 4 pints

8 pounds tomatoes
4 bell peppers
4 Bermuda onions
3 garlic cloves
3 cups apple-cider vinegar
3 cups granulated sugar
3 tablespoons noniodized salt
1 tablespoon dry mustard
¼ teaspoon cayenne pepper
½ teaspoon whole allspice
1 teaspoon whole cloves
1 stick cinnamon, broken into 3
      pieces

Peel and seed tomatoes; cut into quarters.
Seed green peppers; cut into strips.
Peel and quarter onions.
Peel garlic.
Chop vegetables fine, using food processor or blender. Add vinegar, sugar, salt, mustard, and cayenne pepper; mix well.
Tie remaining spices in cheesecloth bag; add to above mixture. Place in Dutch oven; place over grill. Cover. (Or place in slow cooker; cover.) Cook until volume is reduced by one-half. Remove spice bag.
Pour catsup into sterilized jars; process in boiling-water bath 15 minutes. Cook completely. Make sure jars have sealed before storing.

Picture on opposite page: farm catsup

tomato–mustard sauce

Delicious with hamburgers.

Yield: 1½ cups

2 tablespoons minced onion
¼ cup minced celery
2 tablespoons olive oil
2 tablespoons flour
2 tablespoons prepared mustard
1 teaspoon salt
Dash of pepper
1¾ cups canned tomatoes,
   strained

Cook onion and celery in olive oil until transparent. Add flour; mix until smooth. Add mustard, salt, and pepper. Gradually add tomatoes; cook over low heat until mixture boils and thickens.

pork barbecue sauce

Use sauce to baste pork.

Yield: Approximately 1½ cups

2 tablespoons butter
1 medium onion, chopped
2 teaspoons salt
½ teaspoon pepper
1 cup tomato sauce
1 tablespoon lemon juice
1 tablespoon sugar
1 tablespoon Worcestershire sauce
1 teaspoon dry mustard
1 teaspoon garlic powder

Melt butter in heavy saucepan. Sauté onions until soft. Add remaining ingredients; mix well. Heat thoroughly.

backyard barbecue sauce

Yield: 3¾ cups

1 can beer
½ cup lemon juice
¼ tablespoon Worcestershire
    sauce
2 cups chili sauce

Combine all ingredients in saucepan. Place on grill; bring to boil. Move to edge of grill; keep warm while using to baste.

down-home barbecue sauce

Use this as a marinade and/or basting sauce.

Yield: Approximately 1¾ cups

¼ cup vegetable oil
⅓ cup apple-cider vinegar
½ cup orange juice
½ cup catsup
1 medium onion, minced
⅓ cup Worcestershire sauce
1 teaspoon garlic salt
1 teaspoon celery salt
1 teaspoon chili powder
Dash of cayenne pepper

Combine all ingredients in saucepan; bring to boil. Simmer 10 minutes.

tomato barbecue sauce

tomato barbecue sauce

Yield: 1½ cups

½ cup vegetable oil
⅓ cup red-wine vinegar
¼ cup molasses
½ cup catsup
1 tablespoon lemon juice
1 tablespoon Worcestershire sauce
1 teaspoon dry mustard
1 small onion, finely chopped
1 teaspoon garlic powder

Combine all ingredients in heavy saucepan; bring to boil. Reduce heat; simmer ½ hour. Use warm.

summer barbecue sauce

This all-purpose sauce is good for marinating meat or to brush meat while cooking.

Yield: 1 quart

½ cup butter
1 garlic clove, minced
1 large onion, minced
Dash of hot sauce
½ cup catsup
1 teaspoon dry mustard
2 tablespoons prepared
    horseradish
1 tablespoon Worcestershire sauce
2 tablespoons apple-cider vinegar
1 tablespoon brown sugar
1 teaspoon chili powder
1 teaspoon salt
½ teaspoon marjoram
½ teaspoon thyme
¼ teaspoon pepper
3 cups water

Combine all ingredients in heavy saucepan; simmer 30 minutes. Refrigerate if not used immediately.

the working-woman's barbecue sauce

This recipe stores well in the refrigerator.

Yield: 3 cups

1 cup molasses
1 cup prepared spicy mustard
1 cup red-wine vinegar

Blend molasses and mustard in blender. Add vinegar; continue blending, just enough to mix. Refrigerate.

sauce for smoked turkey

Yield: 1 cup

1 cup sour cream
1½ tablespoons tarragon
1 tablespoon lemon juice
½ teaspoon salt

sauce for smoked turkey

Combine ingredients; blend thoroughly. Refrigerate 4 hours before serving.

cucumber–yogurt sauce

A delicious sauce for fowl or fish.

Yield: 1½ cups

1½ cups plain yogurt   **1 teaspoon salt**
½ teaspoon garlic powder   **1 cucumber, pureed**

Combine all ingredients; mix well.

horseradish sauce

Serve this with your favorite grilled steak.

Yield: ¾ cup

½ cup sour cream
2 tablespoons mayonnaise
2 tablespoons prepared
**   horseradish**
½ teaspoon salt
⅛ teaspoon white pepper

Combine ingredients; blend.

lamb honey–mustard glaze

Use to baste lamb during last 30 minutes of cooking.

Yield: 1 cup

½ cup spicy mustard
½ cup apple-blossom honey
Dash of nutmeg

Combine all ingredients; blend well.

lamb orange – marmalade glaze

Use to baste lamb during last 30 minutes of cooking.

Yield: ¾ cup

½ cup English bitter orange
    marmalade
¼ cup lemon juice
1 teaspoon crushed rosemary
    leaves

Combine ingredients; mix well.

garlic butter for steaks

Yield: ½ cup

1 stick butter
1 teaspoon dry mustard
1 teaspoon salt
1 teaspoon paprika
½ teaspoon garlic powder
1 tablespoon Worcestershire sauce
1 teaspoon prepared horseradish

Soften butter. Add remaining ingredients; work with your hands until well-blended.

blue — cheese spread

Yield: ½ cup

½ cup crumbled blue cheese
2 tablespoons margarine, softened

Combine ingredients; mix well. Spreads best at room temperature.

chive butter

Yield: ½ cup

1 stick butter, softened
3 tablespoons finely chopped fresh chives

Place ingredients into small bowl. Work with your hands until well-blended. Wrap butter in waxed paper that has been moistened with cold water. Chill. To serve, unwrap and slice.

chive butter

corned-beef treats

Yield: 24 appetizers

1 12-ounce can corned beef
12 strips bacon
¼ cup pineapple juice
¼ cup butter, melted

Slice corned beef into 4 thick slices. Cut each slice into 6 chunks.
Cut strips of bacon in half lengthwise. Wrap each corned-beef cube with a bacon strip. Place on skewer.
Combine pineapple juice and butter. Baste meat.
Grill meat over hot coals 8 to 10 minutes, basting and turning frequently.

broiled chicken livers

Yield: 4 servings

12 chicken livers
8 slices bacon
12 mushroom caps
¼ cup butter, melted
Freshly grated pepper
Salt

Cut chicken livers in half.
Using 1 bacon slice, 6 chicken-liver halves, and 3 mushrooms per skewer, weave bacon slice onto skewer, alternating chicken livers and mushrooms between folds. Brush with melted butter; sprinkle with pepper and salt. Grill over hot coals 5 minutes or until done. Serve immediately.

chicken livers teriyaki

Yield: 4 servings

16 chicken livers
½ cup Teriyaki Sauce
Hot mustard sauce

Place chicken livers in shallow pan; cover with boiling water. Simmer 4 minutes. Drain. Cover livers with Teriyaki Sauce; marinate 4 hours.

Place livers on individual skewers; grill about 2 minutes. Serve with hot mustard sauce.

teriyaki sauce

Yield: ½ cup

½ cup soy sauce
¼ teaspoon salt
Dash of white pepper
1 tablespoon sugar
½ teaspoon monosodium glutamate
½ teaspoon allspice
¼ teaspoon ground ginger

Combine all ingredients in small saucepan. Heat to boiling.

olive–steak kebabs

A delicious blend of flavors.

Yield: 12 appetizers

12 small steak strips cut from sirloin
12 large olives, stuffed with almonds
¼ cup steak sauce

Wrap steak strips around olives; fasten with toothpicks.

Arrange steak kebabs and steak sauce around a small grill. Allow guests to grill their own kebabs and coat with steak sauce.

grilled swedish meatballs

Yield: 48 meatballs

1 pound ground beef
¼ pound ground veal
¼ pound ground pork
2 cups fresh bread crumbs
½ cup milk
1 onion, finely chopped
2 tablespoons oil
2 teaspoons salt
¼ teaspoon pepper
1 teaspoon nutmeg
1 teaspoon paprika
1 teaspoon dry mustard
3 eggs, beaten

grilled swedish meatballs

Mix meats together, or have butcher grind them together.
Soak bread crumbs in milk. Add meat; mix well.
Sauté onion in 2 tablespoons oil in large skillet.
Mix together seasonings, eggs, onion, and meat in bowl; mix well. Form into 48 small balls. Thread on skewers; grill over hot coals about 5 minutes or until desired doneness is reached.
Serve with Swedish Sauce for dunking.

swedish sauce

¼ teaspoon garlic powder
¼ cup butter
1 tablespoon tomato paste
1 beef bouillon cube
1 cup beef broth
1 cup sour cream

Combine first 5 ingredients in heat-proof casserole. Place over hot coals; simmer until mixture thickens. When meatballs are done, stir sour cream into sauce.
To serve, place sauce in bowl; arrange meatballs around sauce.
Sauce can be made the day before and reheated on grill while meatballs are cooking.

mushroom caps

Yield: 24 appetizers

24 fresh mushroom caps
⅔ cup mayonnaise
¼ cup grated Parmesan cheese
¼ teaspoon garlic powder
¼ teaspoon paprika

Wash mushroom caps; let dry on paper towel.

Combine mayonnaise, cheese, and garlic powder; mix well. Fill mushroom caps with cheese mixture; sprinkle with paprika. Arrange mushrooms around perimeter of grill*; grill 8 minutes. Serve immediately.

* Do not place directly over coals. Mushroom cap will cook before filling is heated thoroughly.

steak kebabs with dunking sauce

This appetizer can be cooked quickly on the grill before you start grilling the main course, or at the same time if needed.

Yield: 6 servings

1 pound boneless sirloin steak
¾ cup red wine
3 tablespoons vegetable oil

1 tablespoon soy sauce
1 teaspoon garlic powder
Dunking Sauce

Cut steak into bite-size pieces.

Combine red wine, vegetable oil, soy sauce, and garlic powder in bowl; mix well. Add meat cubes. Cover; marinate in refrigerator overnight.

Thread cubes on skewer; grill 3 to 5 minutes or until desired degree of doneness is reached. Remove from skewers.

Serve with Dunking Sauce for a delicious appetizer.

dunking sauce

Yield: 1 cup

1 cup tomato catsup
2 tablespoons prepared
   horseradish

Combine catsup and horseradish; mix thoroughly. Serve with steak kebabs.

steak kebabs with dunking sauce

grilled shrimp with bacon

Yield: 16 appetizers

16 peeled and deveined shrimp
16 slices bacon

Wrap shrimp with bacon; secure with toothpicks. Place on grill over hot coals; cook 5 to 6 minutes, turning once during cooking period. Serve immediately.

21

hawaiian rumaki

hawaiian rumaki

Yield: 27 appetizers

9 slices bacon
27 small water chestnuts
27 thin slices tenderloin
Soy sauce

Cut bacon into thirds. Wrap each strip of bacon around a chestnut and a small slice of tenderloin. Baste with soy sauce.

To serve, arrange appetizers around small grill. Pour soy sauce into small bowl; set by grill. Let guests fix their own appetizers as desired.

piedmont fondue

Yield: 6 servings

½ cup butter
½ cup olive oil
4 garlic cloves, peeled, finely
    minced
1 2-ounce can anchovies, drained,
    finely chopped
¼ teaspoon freshly ground pepper
10 cups assorted raw vegetables,
    peeled, trimmed, cut up
1 loaf French bread, sliced

piedmont fondue

Heat butter and olive oil together 6 inches from grill. (Do not brown butter.) Add garlic, anchovies, and pepper. Heat until mixture bubbles and anchovies dissolve. Pour into fondue pot; keep warm throughout serving period.

Arrange vegetables around fondue pot. Provide guests with forks to spear vegetables, swirl in sauce, and eat holding bread like a napkin under vegetables.

chili and cheese dip

Yield: 6 to 8 servings

1 pound pasteurized processed
    American-cheese spread
½ cup prepared taco sauce
Corn chips

Dice cheese into small cubes. Place in ceramic dish; cover. Place ceramic dish in pan of water on grill; heat until cheese melts. Stir in taco sauce.

Serve dip in chafing dish, so that dip remains warm. Serve with corn chips.

oriental soup

A unique appetizer for an outdoor picnic.

Yield: 4 servings

1 quart chicken broth
1 small onion, thinly sliced
¼ cup bamboo shoots, cut into
**   thin strips**
12 whole, peeled, cooked shrimp
2 chicken breasts, skinned,
**   cooked, cut into strips**
½ teaspoon soy sauce

Heat chicken broth over hot coals. Add onion; simmer 10 minutes. Add remaining ingredients; simmer 5 more minutes or until ingredients are heated thoroughly.

oriental soup

cream of tomato soup

A quick appetizer for a backyard barbecue.

Yield: 3 cups

**2 10¾-ounce cans cream of tomato
soup
1 soup-can hot water
¼ cup sour cream
Parsley flakes**

Combine soup and water in heat-proof container without wood or plastic handle. (A cast-iron Dutch oven works well.) Place over hot bed of coals (about 3 to 4 inches from coals); heat thoroughly. Stir soup during cooking process, to prevent scorching.

Ladle soup into serving bowls; garnish with sour cream and parsley.

french-bread fondue

Yield: 16 servings

**1 cup white wine (Chablis or
California white wine)
2 whole garlic cloves, peeled
¾ pound Swiss cheese, grated
3 tablespoons flour
Freshly ground black pepper
3 tablespoons kirsch
3 tablespoons butter
¼ cup heavy cream
1 teaspoon salt
1 loaf Sourdough French Bread
(see Index)**

Pour wine into 1½-quart heat-proof casserole. Add garlic. Simmer, uncovered, over hot coals 10 minutes. Remove; discard garlic.

Combine cheese, flour, and pepper. Stir into hot wine; simmer 10 minutes. Stir in kirsch, butter, and cream; simmer 15 more minutes. Season with salt.

Cube bread; serve with fondue.

variety meats and eggs

chili–cheese casserole

A delicious casserole to fix when camping, because it takes very little of your precious refrigerator space.

Yield: 4 servings

2 cups crushed corn chips
2 16-ounce cans chili with beans
½ cup chopped onions
½ cup chopped green peppers
1 cup grated cheddar cheese

Layer ingredients in greased heat-proof casserole dish, beginning with crushed corn chips and ending with cheese. Cover with aluminum foil. Bake by indirect method (see Index) over hot coals 1 hour or until heated thoroughly and cheese melts.

frank and bacon twirls

Yield: 4 servings

4 frankfurters
4 ounces cheddar cheese
1 tablespoon prepared mustard
4 slices bacon
4 frankfurter buns

Slice frankfurters in half lengthwise.
Grate cheese. Add mustard to cheese; mix well. Spread cheese mixture between frankfurter halves. Wrap 1 bacon strip around each frankfurter; fasten with toothpicks. Place on grill over hot coals; cook until bacon is crisp and franks are thoroughly heated, about 10 minutes.
Toast buns on grill. Serve frankfurters in toasted buns.

johnnie's catsup franks

Yield: 4 servings

1 cup catsup
8 all-beef frankfurters

Heat catsup in large cast-iron skillet over hot coals. Add hot dogs; simmer 30 minutes or until catsup thickens and darkens and frankfurters are thoroughly heated.

chili franks

Yield: 8 servings

8 frankfurters
1 cup chili without beans
8 frankfurter buns
¼ cup finely chopped onions

Place frankfurters on grill over hot coals; cook 6 minutes, turning frequently to ensure even cooking.

Pour chili into shallow pan; place on grill. Heat thoroughly, about 6 minutes.

Place cooked franks in buns; top with heated chili and chopped onions.

pigs in blanket

Yield: 4 servings

1¼ cups prepared biscuit mix
⅓ cup milk
4 frankfurters

Make rolled biscuit dough as directed on package, reducing milk to ⅓ cup.

On floured board roll dough to ⅛ inch thick. Cut into 4 3½-inch squares. Place a frankfurter in center of each square; wrap meat with dough. Place covered frankfurter on stick or skewer; grill over hot coals until dough is brown on each side.

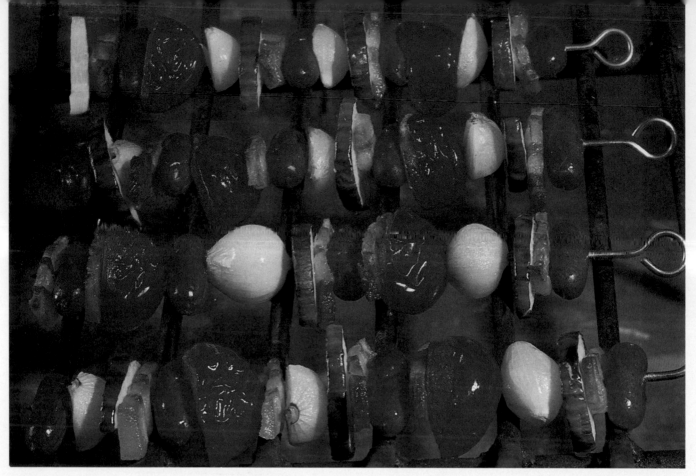

frankfurter kebabs

frankfurter kebabs

Yield: 4 servings

4 small tomatoes
4 strips thick (country-style) bacon
8 small white onions
1 large cucumber
16 cocktail frankfurters
¼ cup vegetable oil
¼ cup lemon juice
Dash of thyme
½ teaspoon dry mustard
2 tablespoons lime juice
¼ teaspoon hot sauce
¼ teaspoon salt

Cut tomatoes in half.
Cut bacon strips into 2-inch pieces.
Peel and halve onions if too large.
Slice cucumber into thick slices.
Arrange vegetables and meat on skewers in alternate layers.
Combine remaining ingredients; mix well. Brush kebabs with sauce. Place kebabs on grill over hot coals; cook 15 minutes, basting and turning frequently.

28

the all-american hot dog

Yield: 4 servings

4 all-beef hot dogs
4 buns
Catsup
Mustard

Relish
Chopped onions
French-Fried Onion Rings (see Index)

Place hot dogs on cooking grill; cook 6 to 8 minutes, turning every 2 minutes. Remove from grill.

Serve hot dogs in buns garnished with catsup, mustard, relish, and chopped onions. Top with French-Fried Onion Rings if desired.

the all-american hot dog

grilled corned-beef hash with eggs

A delicious breakfast for a lazy summer morning.

Yield: 8 servings

3 cups mashed potatoes
2¼ cups shredded canned corned
beef
2 tablespoons tomato puree
Dash of pepper
4 eggs, beaten
Poached Eggs

Combine potatoes, corned beef, tomato puree, pepper, and uncooked eggs; mix to combine. Shape into patties. Place on shallow dish; cover with plastic wrap. Refrigerate overnight.

Place patties on grill over hot coals. Grill about 4 minutes on each side or until heated thoroughly. Be careful when turning patties. Serve with Poached Eggs.

poached eggs

Yield: 8 servings

8 eggs
Salt
Pepper

In shallow pan bring 2 inches water to simmer.

Break eggs, 1 at a time, into cup; transfer to water by holding cup with egg on surface of water; gently pour egg into water. Cook 3 to 5 minutes, to desired degree of doneness. Remove from water with slotted spoon; sprinkle with salt and pepper.

grilled corned-beef hash with eggs

italian sausage with tomato sauce

Yield: 4 servings

**2 pounds sweet Italian sausage
1 8-ounce jar spaghetti sauce
4 hard rolls**

Place sausage on grill, directly over hot coals. Brown evenly on all sides, about 15 minutes. Move sausage to outside of grill or raise grill 6 inches from coals; grill 20 additional minutes.

Pour spaghetti sauce into shallow heat-proof bowl. Place on grill; cook until volume is reduced by ½.

Place cooked sausage in hard rolls; spoon spaghetti sauce over sausage.

sausage and potato fry

Yield: 4 servings

1 pound sausage in casings
4 large potatoes, peeled, sliced

Slice sausage; fry in large skillet over hot coals. Remove sausage from skillet.

Add potatoes to skillet. Fry on 1 side without stirring. When done on 1 side, use pancake turner to flip potatoes with 1 turn. Fry remaining side until done. Add sausage to potatoes.

Garnish with parsley. Serve.

sausage and potato fry

liver and ham kebabs

By using frozen liver slices, you need not devein the liver.

Yield: 6 servings

1 to 1½ pounds frozen calves-liver slices
½ pound ham, sliced thick
30 large mushroom caps
¼ cup butter, melted
½ teaspoon salt
¼ teaspoon freshly ground pepper
2 large apples

Thaw liver slightly. Cut into 2-inch chunks.
Slice ham into 2-inch chunks.
Clean mushrooms.
Arrange meat and mushrooms on skewers.
Combine butter, salt, and pepper. Baste kebabs. Place kebabs on grill; grill until done, about 3 to 4 minutes each side. Baste kebabs when you turn them.
Core apples; slice into rings. Place apple rings on grill; cook until peel starts to curl.
To serve, arrange apple slices on platter; top with kebabs.

camping bacon and eggs

Yield: 4 servings

8 slices white bread
2 tablespoons butter, softened
4 hard-cooked eggs, sliced
    diagonally
1 teaspoon salt
¼ teaspoon white pepper
4 slices bacon, cut in half
    crosswise

Spread each bread slice with butter. Arrange sliced eggs on half of bread slices. Sprinkle with salt and pepper. Top with remaining bread slices, butter-side-down. Place sandwiches in long-handled, hinged wire broiler or toaster; top each with 2 half-slices bacon, side by side. Brown both sides of sandwiches over hot coals, leaving side with bacon until last. Serve hot.

hole — in — one eggs

Yield: 6 servings

Oil for frying
6 1-inch-thick slices homemade
    bread
1 teaspoon salt
¼ teaspoon pepper
6 eggs

Place cast-iron skillet on top of grill approximately 2 inches from hot coals. Pour frying oil into skillet; heat thoroughly.

Cut centers from bread slices, using doughnut cutter. (Use centers for making croutons.) Place prepared bread in heated skillet.

Break an egg. Pour it in center of bread slice. Fry until bread is browned and egg white is cooked. Turn bread and egg at same time. Fry remaining side to desired doneness. Sprinkle with salt and pepper. Prepare remaining servings in same manner. Replenish oil in skillet as needed. Preheat oil each time before frying bread.

ham egg nest

A quick breakfast when you must get up early to start your trip home after an enjoyable camping trip.

Yield: 4 servings

1 can (12 ounces) ham loaf
2 tablespoons oil
4 eggs

Cut loaf into 4 ½-inch-thick slices. Cut square hole in middle of each slice. Pour oil into skillet; heat over hot coals. Brown cut-out ham pieces on each side; keep warm. Brown large pieces of meat on 1 side. Turn meat. Break egg into cut-out center of each ham slice. Cover; cook egg to desired degree of doneness.

beef

grilled steaks

Have a large enough fire to cook steaks quickly; however, do not place steaks on coals until fire has died down and coals are red-hot.

Steaks should be grilled 4 to 5 inches from the coals. The thicker the steaks or the more well-done you want them, the farther they should be placed from the coals.

Choose top-quality steaks, at least 1 inch thick. Porterhouse, T-bone, sirloin, or filet are good choices.

Score the visible fat every 1 inch to prevent curling. Broil one side until well-browned before turning. Turn with tongs to prevent juices from escaping from the heat. Grill remaining side to desired degree of doneness.

Steak Thickness	Rare	Medium	Well-Done
1 inch	6–8 minutes	8–10 minutes	12–15 minutes
2 inches	15–17 minutes	18–20 minutes	21–24 minutes

grilled steaks

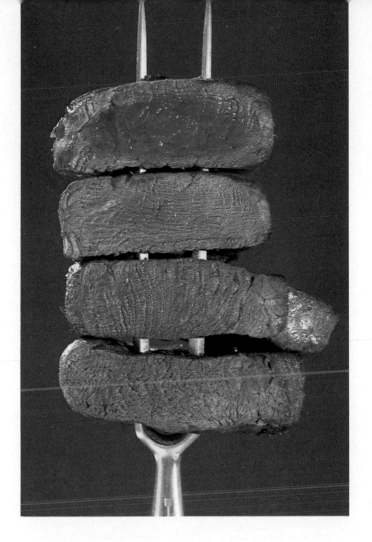

degrees of doneness—beef

Top: *Rare*
      Medium Rare
      Medium

Bottom: *Well-Done*

marinated chuck steak

A less tender cut of meat can be cooked over coals, if first marinated to tenderize the meat.

Yield: 4 servings

1 clove garlic, minced	**2 tablespoons lemon juice**
1 teaspoon ground black pepper	**¼ cup olive oil**
1 bay leaf	**2½ to 3 pounds chuck steak, ¾**
1 cup red wine	**inch thick**

Combine all ingredients except steak. Pour over steak in shallow pan. Let stand at room temperature about 4 hours, turning steak several times.

Remove steak from sauce; place over hot coals. Cook steak to desired doneness, turning once. Baste with sauce while cooking.

grilled loin steaks with herb butter

The Herb Butter may be made ahead and frozen for later use.

4 8-ounce boneless loin steaks
Salt
Freshly ground pepper

Slit any visible fat at 1-inch intervals to prevent fat from curling during grilling. Sprinkle both sides of steaks with salt and pepper. Place on grill 5 inches from hot coals; grill 8 minutes on each side for rare, 9 minutes on each side for medium, and 12 minutes on each side for well-done.

herb butter

½ cup (1 stick) butter
3 tablespoons fresh chives
½ teaspoon salt

Place ingredients in bowl; work with your hands to mix well. Wrap prepared Herb Butter in waxed paper lightly moistened with cold water. Form into roll; chill until hard.

Just before serving, remove from refrigerator; slice. Serve on top of steak or pass on separate dish.

lemon-flavored steaks

Yield: 4 servings

4 8-ounce loin steaks
Freshly ground pepper
1 clove garlic, crushed
2 tablespoons fresh-squeezed
    lemon juice
½ teaspoon salt
1 teaspoon oregano

Rub meat with pepper and garlic. Place on grill over hot coals; grill to desired degree of doneness. Remove from grill; sprinkle with lemon juice, salt, and oregano.

cowboy steak

cowboy steak

A version of the meals eaten by wild-west cowboys.

Yield: 2 servings

4 strips bacon
2 8-ounce eye-of-the-round steaks
Salt and pepper
2 cups pork and beans

Heat large skillet over hot coals. Fry bacon until crisp. Remove.
Place steaks in skillet. Sprinkle with salt and pepper. Fry to desired degree of doneness.
During last 10 minutes of cooking period, heat beans in skillet.

"cook-your-own" cookout

Yield: 6 servings

1 pound sirloin steak
1 pound chicken breasts
1 pound weiners
2 dozen cherry tomatoes
2 dozen pearl onions, cleaned
2 green peppers, cut into wedges
1 cup soy sauce
½ teaspoon Tabasco

Slice sirloin steak and chicken breasts into wafer-thin slices.
Cut weiners into 1-inch chunks.
Arrange meat and vegetables on large platter, and place on crushed-ice bed to prevent food from spoiling during hot weather.
Combine soy sauce and Tabasco; divide into 6 dishes.
Let each guest cook his food to desired doneness over hot coals and dip in his own dunking dish.

tenderloin on a spit

A meat thermometer is essential for this expensive cut of meat to ensure cooking it to perfection.

Yield: 10 to 12 servings

1 5- to 6-pound beef tenderloin
1 teaspoon salt
¼ teaspoon freshly ground pepper
½ cup melted butter
Orange Cups (see Index)

Buy a whole tenderloin; leave it in 1 piece. Remove excess fat. Fold slender tips back; hold in place with metal skewers or tie with twine. Pierce meat lengthwise with rod of spit. Secure on rotisserie as directed by manufacturer. Rub with salt and pepper. Insert meat thermometer. Grill over hot coals, basting with butter at beginning and at 15 minute intervals thereafter. Cook to desired degree of doneness. Allow to stand 30 minutes before carving.

To serve, arrange meat on serving platter; garnish with Orange Cups.

Picture on opposite page: tenderloin on a spit

beef cubes with peanut-butter sauce

A delicious version of the famous beef satay served in Australia.

Yield: 4 servings

1 pound sirloin steak
1 onion
1 teaspoon ground ginger
½ cup finely chopped unsalted
    roasted peanuts
2 tablespoons granulated sugar
1 teaspoon salt
1 teaspoon caraway seeds
½ teaspoon garlic powder

Cut steak into 1-inch cubes.

Grate onion; mix with ginger, peanuts, sugar, salt, caraway seeds, and garlic powder. Stir in steak cubes. Marinate in refrigerator 24 hours.

Distribute marinated meat cubes among 8 metal skewers. Broil over hot coals, turning frequently, 25 to 30 minutes or until cooked to desired degree of doneness.

Serve beef over rice, with Peanut-Butter Sauce.

peanut-butter sauce

1 tablespoon butter
1 onion, finely chopped
1 teaspoon garlic powder
½ teaspoon Mexican-style chili
    powder
¾ cup water
⅓ cup crunchy peanut butter
1 teaspoon honey

Melt butter in saucepan over hot coals. Add onion; cook until transparent. Add remaining ingredients; heat thoroughly.

sukiyaki

Oriental cuisine lends itself to outdoor cooking. One of the leading kettle manufacturers even makes a wok that fits over the hot coals.

To cook sukiyaki, fill a hibachi with coals; let coals get red-hot before preparing your meal.

Yield: 4 servings

2 pounds beef tenderloin
½ pound transparent noodles
1 cup sliced fresh mushrooms
4 small onions, thinly sliced
6 spring onions, thinly sliced
½ pound cabbage, chopped into
    bite-size pieces
½ pound spinach leaves, chopped
1 cup canned bamboo shoots,
    drained
2 cups canned bean sprouts,
    drained

sauce

1 cup soy sauce
⅓ cup rice wine
1 tablespoon sugar

4 egg yolks
4 cups cooked rice
2 tablespoons bacon drippings

Cut beef tenderloin into paper-thin slices (beef is easier to cut when partially frozen). Place on serving platter. Cover; refrigerate.

Cover noodles with boiling water; soak 25 minutes. Repeat process 2 more times. Drain. Place in serving bowl.

Arrange vegetables in serving bowls.

Combine sauce ingredients; bring to boil. Pour into serving dish.

Divide egg yolks into 4 serving bowls.

Divide rice into 4 serving dishes.

Place hibachi with hot coals in center of picnic table. Place frying pan on top hot coals. Arrange ingredients around wok, being sure each guest has a bowl of rice and a bowl of egg yolk.

Prepare meal in portions. Place one-fourth of bacon drippings into pan; heat. Add one-fourth of meat slices; brown quickly. Push to one side; pour a small amount of sauce over meat. Add one-fourth of each vegetable; cook quickly, stirring constantly, about 4 minutes.

Dip cooked vegetables in egg yolk before serving to guests. Cook remaining food in same manner, serving each guest a portion of cooked food each time.

Picture on following pages: sukiyaki

cheeseburgers

Yield: 4 servings

1 pound ground beef
½ teaspoon salt
Dash of pepper
1 tablespoon Worcestershire sauce
1 teaspoon dry mustard
4 cherry tomatoes
4 slices American cheese
4 hamburger buns
Lettuce
Catsup
Mustard

Combine beef, salt, pepper, Worcestershire sauce, and dry mustard; mix well. Form into 4 patties. Place on grill over hot coals; grill 4 minutes on first side. Turn hamburgers; grill remaining side 4 minutes.

Halve cherry tomatoes; place on top of patties.

Slice cheese into strips; place on top of tomatoes. Grill 2 minutes. Remove from grill.

Serve cheeseburgers on buns, garnished with lettuce, catsup, and mustard.

cheeseburgers

pizza burgers

The sauce can be made ahead and warmed on the grill.

Yield: 6 servings

1½ pounds ground beef
½ cup chopped onion
¾ teaspoon garlic salt
¼ teaspoon pepper
8 ounces mozzarella cheese, sliced

sauce

2 cups peeled Italian-style
    tomatoes, broken with fork
1 8-ounce can tomato sauce
¼ cup mushroom stems and
    pieces
1 teaspoon crushed dried oregano
1 teaspoon garlic powder

6 English muffins

Combine ground beef, onion, garlic salt, and pepper. Form into 6 oblong patties. Grill over hot coals 5 minutes on each side. Top with cheese; grill 2 minutes.

To make sauce, combine tomatoes, tomato sauce, mushrooms, oregano, and garlic powder in saucepan; heat.

Place cooked patties on English-muffin rounds; top with sauce.

blue-cheese burgers

Yield: 4 servings

1 pound ground beef
1 small onion, chopped
1 teaspoon salt
¼ teaspoon pepper
¼ cup blue cheese
2 tablespoons mayonnaise

Combine ground beef, onion, salt, and pepper; mix well. Form into 8 thin patties.

Combine blue cheese and mayonnaise. Spread evenly over 4 patties. Top with remaining 4 patties. Seal edges. Grill hamburgers 5 minutes per side.

Serve burgers on buns.

mexican hamburger steaks

Yield: 4 servings

1 pound ground chuck
2 tablespoons canned chopped
**   green chilies**
1 onion, finely chopped
1 teaspoon salt
½ teaspoon garlic powder
¼ teaspoon black pepper

Lightly combine all ingredients in mixing bowl. Form into 4 thick patties. Place on grill 4 to 5 inches from coals; cook to desired degree of doneness. Turn hamburgers halfway through the cooking period.

Rare: 6–8 minutes
Medium: 9–10 minutes
Well Done: 11–12 minutes

veal dogs

When the children ask for hot dogs for the next outdoor cookout, treat the adults to this unusual recipe.

Yield: 4 dogs

¼ **pound ground veal**
¼ **pound ground pork**
¼ **cup onion, finely chopped**
1 egg white
1 teaspoon salt
¼ **teaspoon white pepper**

Mix ingredients together thoroughly. Shape into 4 oblong patties. Grill over hot coals approximately 8 minutes on each side or until cooked thoroughly. (Since pork is in mixture, meat must be cooked all the way through.)
Serve veal dogs in hot-dog buns.

sloppy joes

A delicious dish to serve at a fund-raiser when no gas or electricity is available.

Yield: 6 servings

1½ pounds ground beef
1 onion, chopped
1 green pepper, diced fine
¾ **cup catsup**
¼ **cup water**
2 tablespoons brown sugar
2 teaspoons Worcestershire sauce
1 tablespoon prepared mustard
1 teaspoon salt
1 teaspoon garlic powder
6 hamburger buns

Place meat in heat-proof casserole or cast-iron skillet. Place over hot coals; cook 30 minutes or until browned. Add onion and green pepper; cook over hot coals until vegetables are soft. Add remaining ingredients; mix well. Move to one side of grill; simmer 20 minutes to combine flavors. Stir occasionally to prevent sticking.
Serve this over split hamburger buns.

meat loaf supreme

Next time you light up the charcoals for a hamburger or hot-dog cookout, utilize the coals to the fullest by baking a meat loaf to be served the next day. All you need do is reheat the cooked loaf in a conventional oven; or, why not serve it sliced cold for Dad's poker night?

Yield: 4 servings

1 pound ground beef
3 tablespoons chili sauce
2 teaspoons prepared mustard
1½ teaspoons horseradish
1 small onion, finely chopped
1 teaspoon salt
½ cup oatmeal
1 egg, beaten
2 teaspoons Worcestershire sauce

Combine all ingredients. Form meat loaf. Place meat loaf in shallow pan; place over drip pan. Cover; cook 1 hour or until done.

bandit pork

Yield: 4 servings

4 pieces heavy-duty foil, 15 inches long	2 medium zucchini squash, sliced
4 medium potatoes, peeled, thinly sliced	½ teaspoon garlic powder
	1 teaspoon salt
4 4-ounce pork chops	½ teaspoon pepper
2 onions, sliced into rings	½ teaspoon oregano
4 carrots, peeled, sliced	2 tablespoons lemon juice
2 stalks celery, thinly sliced	¾ cup Kasseri cheese, grated
	2 tablespoons butter

On each sheet of foil arrange ¼ of sliced potatoes. Top with chop and ¼ of onions, carrots, celery, and squash. Sprinkle with garlic, salt, pepper, oregano, and lemon juice. Top with cheese; dot with butter. Bring up edges of foil; fold to enclose meat and vegetables. Fold ends to seal. Place foil pouches on grill over hot coals, potato-side-down; grill 2 hours or until done.

Serve meat and vegetables from packets.

bandit pork

spit-roasted pork

Yield: 8 servings

1¾ cups red wine
2 tablespoons lemon juice
1 clove garlic, minced
1 medium onion, chopped
½ teaspoon pepper
1 teaspoon crushed coriander
1 4-pound pork loin roast

Combine wine, lemon juice, garlic, onion, pepper, and coriander. Pour into glass or ceramic container about size of pork roast. Add roast; cover. Marinate in refrigerator 24 hours.

Remove from marinade; save marinade. Arrange roast on spit, following manufacturer's instructions. Insert meat thermometer; grill until internal temperature reaches 185°F (about 3 hours). Baste with marinade frequently during cooking process. Let stand 30 minutes before slicing.

spareribs with italian sauce

Yield: 4 servings

4 pounds spareribs
¼ cup vinegar
¾ cup olive oil
¾ cup brown sugar, firmly
    packed
¾ cup tomato catsup
1 cup water

½ teaspoon salt
Dash of white pepper
1½ teaspoons ginger
½ teaspoon dry mustard
2 teaspoons whole oregano
1½ teaspoons celery salt
1 teaspoon garlic powder

Have butcher "crack" (saw through bone that connects ribs together, but leave meat intact so ribs remain one large piece of meat) spareribs.

Combine vinegar, olive oil, brown sugar, catsup, and water in small saucepan. Stir in seasonings; mix well. Simmer about 10 minutes, stirring occasionally. Pour marinade over ribs. Cover. Marinate in refrigerator 24 hours.

Place spareribs on grill; grill 1 hour and 20 minutes, turning and basting about every 20 minutes. Serve immediately.

Picture on opposite page: spit-roasted pork

pork kebabs

pork kebabs

Yield: 4 servings

Juice of 1 lime
¼ cup vegetable oil
¼ teaspoon crushed whole
    coriander
¼ cup chopped onion
1 clove garlic, mashed
¼ teaspoon pepper
1¼ pounds lean pork, cut into
    1½-inch cubes

2 medium cucumbers, sliced
2 red peppers, stemmed, seeded,
    cut into chunks
½ pound fresh mushrooms,
    cleaned
½ cup small cocktail onions

The day before cooking, combine lime juice, oil, coriander, onion, garlic, and pepper in glass bowl. Add pork cubes; mix well. Cover; marinate in refrigerator 24 hours.

Drain meat; reserve marinade. Skewer meat alternately with cucumber slices, red peppers, mushrooms, and cocktail onions. Grill over hot coals 30 minutes; baste and turn every 6 to 8 minutes.

Serve kebabs with rice.

54

pork and veal burgers

Yield: 4 servings

½ pound fresh ground pork
½ pound fresh ground veal
1 teaspoon salt
¼ teaspoon pepper
¼ cup finely chopped onion
½ cup soft bread crumbs
1 tablespoon Worcestershire sauce

If possible, have butcher grind pork and veal together. Add remaining ingredients; mix well. Form into 4 patties. Grill over hot coals 12 minutes or until done. Turn once during cooking period.

barbecue mexican spareribs

Yield: 8 servings

1 tablespoon olive oil
1 medium onion, chopped
1 clove garlic, peeled, minced
1 fresh chili pepper, stemmed,
      seeded, chopped
½ tablespoon salt
2 large tomatoes, peeled, cut up
2 tablespoons chili powder
2 tablespoons sugar
¼ cup red-wine vinegar
⅓ cup olive oil
¼ cup beer
4 pounds country-style spareribs

Heat 1 tablespoon olive oil. Sauté onion in oil until lightly browned. Add garlic, chili, salt, and tomatoes; simmer until mixture thickens. Add remaining sauce ingredients; cook 8 minutes, stirring constantly. Pour over spareribs; marinate in refrigerator 24 hours.

Grill ribs over hot coals, basting periodically with sauce, until tender, well-browned, and crusty, about 2 hours.

Heat remaining sauce; serve with ribs.

southern-california pork ribs

To shorten grilling time, parboil ribs 20 minutes.

Yield: 6 servings

5 pounds spareribs, cracked
½ cup honey
⅔ cup soy sauce
⅔ cup chili sauce
1 teaspoon dry mustard
1 teaspoon paprika
1 cup lemon juice
Dash of hot sauce
2 teaspoons garlic juice
1 teaspoon salt
1 cup fresh-squeezed orange juice

Parboil ribs 20 minutes. Drain.

Combine remaining ingredients; mix well. Pour over ribs; marinate overnight.

Remove ribs from marinade. Place on grill over hot coals; grill about 1 hour or until ribs are crisp. Baste and turn every 10 minutes.

chinese spareribs

Yield: 4 servings

4 pounds spareribs
2 garlic cloves
¼ cup soy sauce
⅓ cup wine vinegar
2 tablespoons honey
½ cup chicken broth
2 tablespoons sesame-seed oil

Have butcher cut spareribs into single ribs.

Finely chop garlic cloves. Add soy sauce, vinegar, honey, chicken broth, and sesame-seed oil; mix thoroughly. Pour sauce over spareribs; cover. Marinate in refrigerator 24 hours.

Remove ribs from sauce; place on grill. Grill 1 hour and 15 minutes, turning and basting with sauce about every 15 minutes.

chinese spareribs

grilled center ham slice

Yield: 4 servings

1 center-cut ham slice, 1 to 1½
inches thick
1 1-pound can cling-peach halves
in heavy syrup
Dash of cloves
½ cup brown sugar
1 tablespoon cornstarch
1 tablespoon butter

Slash fat on outside of ham steak to prevent curling. Place ham on grill over hot coals; grill 20 minutes on each side.

While meat is grilling, drain peaches. Combine cloves, sugar, and cornstarch. Add to peach juice; cook over low heat, stirring constantly, until thickened.

When ham slices are turned, arrange peach halves on outside of grill. Dot with butter. Heat while grilling second side of ham.

To serve, arrange ham and peaches on serving platter. Pass sauce separately.

spiced ham on rotisserie

Yield: 10 to 12 servings

5-pound canned ham
⅛ teaspoon nutmeg
⅛ teaspoon ground cloves
½ cup orange marmalade
1 tablespoon lemon juice

Place ham in net basket or basket supplied with rotisserie. Insert spit lengthwise through center of meat. Fasten with prongs. Insert meat thermometer into meat. Place rotisserie on grill over hot coals, following manufacturer's instructions. Grill to internal temperature of 135°F (about 1 to 1½ hours).

Combine remaining ingredients; baste ham during last 10 minutes of cooking period. Let stand 30 minutes before slicing.

stuffed ham steak

Yield: 4 servings

2 ham steaks
1 medium onion, finely chopped
½ cup diced celery
2 tablespoons vegetable oil
1½ cups fresh bread cubes
1 tablespoon chopped parsley
½ teaspoon salt
1 egg, slightly beaten

Slash fat around ham steaks; set aside.

Sauté onion and celery in oil 10 minutes. Add bread cubes, parsley, salt, and egg; toss lightly.

Place 1 ham steak in center of large double-thick square of aluminum foil; cover steak with stuffing mixture. Top with second ham steak; if necessary, hold in place with toothpicks. Fold foil into neat sealed package. Place foil package on grill over hot coals; cook 60 minutes or until done. Turn once during cooking process.

texas toast sandwiches

Yield: 6 servings

12 slices ½-inch-thick homemade
    bread
1 pound Danish ham, sliced
1 pound Swiss cheese, shredded
½ cup butter, melted

Place 3 ounces ham on half of bread slices. Top ham with Swiss cheese. Cover with remaining bread slices. Brush outside of bread with melted butter. Place sandwiches in long-handled, hinged wire broiler or toaster. Brown both sides of sandwiches over hot coals. Serve hot.

grilled canadian bacon with yams

Yield: 4 servings

4 whole yams
4 4-ounce slices Canadian bacon

Wrap yams in foil; place on grill over hot coals. Grill 1 to 1½ hours or until fork-tender.

During last 20 minutes of cooking period, place Canadian bacon on grill. Cook until heated thoroughly, about 10 minutes on each side.

open-face ham and mushroom sandwiches

A delicious breakfast meal on your next camping trip.

Yield: 4 servings

4 slices whole-wheat bread
2 tablespoons butter
1 cup sliced mushrooms
4 slices ham
2 tomatoes, sliced thin
4 slices American cheese
2 tablespoons chopped fresh chives

Spread both sides of bread with butter. Arrange mushrooms over bread.

Slice ham into strips; layer over mushrooms. Place tomatoes on top of ham.

Cut cheese into strips; layer on top of tomatoes. Place sandwiches on wire sandwich grill; cook over hot coals until heated thoroughly and cheese begins to melt on top.

Sprinkle sandwiches with fresh chives. Serve.

Picture on opposite page: open-face ham and mushroom sandwiches

lamb

spicy leg of lamb

Yield: 10 servings

2 cloves garlic
1 tablespoon dried oregano
1/8 teaspoon ground cumin
2 teaspoons hot chili powder

1 4- to 5-pound leg of lamb
Salt
Pepper

Peel garlic; mash with oregano and cumin. Stir in chili powder.

Using sharp knife, make incisions all over surface of lamb. Place some spice mixture in each incision. Rub roast with salt and pepper. Using indirect method of cooking (see Index), place lamb in center of grill, over drip pan. Insert meat thermometer into lamb; cover grill. Cook until roast reaches 180°F internal temperature, about 3½ to 4 hours.

spanish lamb chops

Yield: 4 servings

¼ cup olive oil
3 tablespoons lime juice
1 garlic clove, crushed
2 tablespoons grated onion
½ teaspoon salt
⅛ teaspoon pepper
4 1-inch-thick lamb chops

Combine olive oil, lime juice, garlic, onion, salt, and pepper; mix well. Pour mixture over lamb; refrigerate. Marinate 24 hours.

Grill chops over hot coals, about 12 minutes per side. Brush with marinade while cooking.

Heat remaining marinade; serve with chops.

smoked stuffed lamb shoulder

smoked stuffed lamb shoulder

Yield: 6 to 8 servings

1½ pounds pork sausage
1 medium onion, chopped
½ teaspoon garlic powder

1 teaspoon parsley flakes
4- to 5-pound lamb shoulder,
    boned, prepared for rolling

Combine sausage, onion, garlic, and parsley flakes. Mix well.

Flatten roast; spread stuffing mixture over roast. Roll roast tightly; secure with string or skewers. Place roast in smoker*; cook 8 to 10 hours or until done. Let stand 20 minutes before slicing.

* If you do not have a smoker, you can turn your covered grill into a smoker by placing a pan of water in the center of the grill and surrounding the pan with charcoal. Place meat over pan of water; cover. Add charcoal every hour to keep fire hot.

63

greek roast leg of lamb

Yield: 8 servings

1 5- to 6-pound leg of lamb
Olive oil
3 garlic cloves, peeled
½ teaspoon rosemary
Salt
Freshly ground pepper

Wipe meat with damp cloth. Coat meat with olive oil. Make slits in lamb; fill with garlic and rosemary. Dust with salt and freshly ground pepper. Using indirect method of cooking (see Index), place lamb in center of grill over drip pan. Insert meat thermometer into lamb; cover grill. Cook until roast reaches 180°F internal temperature, about 4 hours. Let stand 30 minutes before carving.

greek roast leg of lamb

64

barbecued lamb rib chops

Yield: 4 servings

1 8-ounce bottle Italian salad
dressing
1 6-ounce can tomato paste
4 ¾-inch-thick lamb rib chops

Combine salad dressing and tomato paste; blend. Pour over chops; marinate overnight.

Remove chops from marinade; place on grill over hot coals. Grill 7 minutes. Baste with marinade. Turn chops; grill 7 minutes or until desired degree of doneness is reached.

shish kebab in foil

Yield: 6 servings

1 pound lamb cubes
½ pound cocktail frankfurters
½ pound fresh mushrooms
1 dozen cherry tomatoes
2 tablespoons tomato sauce
2 tablespoons vinegar
2 tablespoons brown sugar
1 teaspoon dry mustard
1 medium onion, finely chopped
2 tablespoons olive oil

Place alternate pieces of lamb, frankfurters, mushrooms, and tomatoes on 6 skewers. Place each filled skewer on large square of foil.

Combine remaining ingredients in saucepan. Bring to boil; simmer 5 minutes. Divide sauce among kebabs. Wrap foil around kebabs, double-folding edges together. Pinch around skewer handles. Place over hot coals; grill 30 minutes, turning every 10 minutes.

Serve kebabs in foil.

boneless lamb cutlets with chili sauce

Yield: 8 servings

1 cup chili sauce
¼ cup finely chopped onions
¼ cup finely chopped green
    pepper
¼ cup vinegar
2 tablespoons olive oil
2 tablespoons brown sugar
1 teaspoon thyme
8 1-inch-thick lamb cutlets

Combine chili sauce, onions, green pepper, vinegar, olive oil, and brown sugar. Simmer gently 10 minutes. Add thyme.

Baste lamb with sauce. Place cutlets on grill over hot coals. Grill 10 minutes. Baste and turn cutlets; grill 10 minutes or until done.

Heat remaining sauce; serve with lamb cutlets.

fruit and lamb kebabs

Yield: 4 servings

1½ pounds lamb cubes
4 bananas
½ cup lemon juice
4 peach halves, drained
8 pitted dates
¼ cup butter
1 teaspoon cinnamon

Arrange lamb on skewers.

Peel bananas; divide each into 4 pieces. Brush with lemon juice. Arrange banana pieces, peaches, and dates on skewers.

Melt butter on grill; stir in cinnamon.

Broil lamb 4 inches from hot coals 10 minutes. Turn. Add fruit skewers to grill. Brush with cinnamon butter. Grill lamb and fruit kebabs 7 to 8 minutes, basting fruit kebabs frequently.

cantonese kebabs

Yield: 4 servings

½ cup soy sauce
½ cup maraschino cherry juice
½ cup red wine
¼ cup apple-blossom honey

1 teaspoon ginger
2 teaspoons garlic powder
¼ cup olive oil
4 pounds lamb riblets

Combine all ingredients except lamb. Pour over lamb; marinate 24 hours.
Drain riblets; place on skewers. Grill over hot coals 45 to 60 minutes, turn-ing and basting frequently during cooking period.
Serve lamb with fruit kebabs.

boneless lamb cutlets with chili sauce

lamb and pepper kebabs

lamb and pepper kebabs

Yield: 4 servings

¼ cup minced onion
¼ cup olive oil
¼ cup lemon juice
1 teaspoon garlic powder
1 teaspoon salt
1½ pounds lamb cubes
2 red peppers
2 bell peppers

Combine onion, olive oil, lemon juice, garlic powder, and salt; mix well. Pour over lamb cubes; marinate overnight in refrigerator.

Drain; reserve marinade.

Remove seeds and stems from peppers; cut into cubes. Alternate layers of lamb cubes and peppers on skewers. Place kebabs on grill over hot coals; grill 10 minutes on each side, basting frequently.

shish kebab with rice pilaf

Yield: 4 servings

¼ cup vinegar
½ cup white wine
2 tablespoons oil
1 teaspoon tarragon
1 teaspoon garlic powder
1 bay leaf
¼ teaspoon mustard seed
2 cloves
1-inch-piece stick cinnamon
¼ teaspoon allspice
¼ teaspoon coriander

¼ teaspoon ginger
Dash of crushed red pepper
4 peppercorns
2 pounds lamb cubes
2 green peppers
2 ripe tomatoes
8 whole mushrooms
¼ cup butter
1 cup rice
¼ cup onions, minced
2 cups chicken stock

Combine vinegar, wine, oil, and spices in shaker; mix well. Pour over lamb; marinate 24 hours.

Drain lamb; reserve marinade.

Seed peppers; slice into wedges.

Cut tomatoes into wedges.

Alternate lamb cubes, green pepper, tomato wedges, and mushrooms on 4 metal skewers. Baste with marinade. Place on grill over hot coals; grill about 20 to 25 minutes or until desired degree of doneness is reached. Baste frequently during cooking period.

Melt butter in Dutch oven. Add rice and onions; cook, stirring constantly, until rice is light brown. Add chicken broth; simmer, covered, 30 minutes or until all liquid is absorbed.

Serve kebabs with rice.

shish kebab with rice pilaf

69

lamb on skewers

Yield: 4 servings

¼ cup minced onion
3 tablespoons olive oil
3 tablespoons lemon juice
1 teaspoon garlic powder
1 teaspoon salt
¼ teaspoon pepper
½ teaspoon dried oregano
1½ pounds lamb cubes
16 pearl onions, peeled
16 mushroom caps
1 cup red-pepper chunks

Combine onion, olive oil, lemon juice, garlic powder, salt, pepper, and oregano; mix well. Add lamb cubes; stir well. Cover; marinate overnight in refrigerator.

Drain lamb; reserve marinade.

Skewer vegetables and lamb alternately. Place on grill over hot bed of coals. Grill 10 to 12 minutes on each side, marinating frequently.

Serve kebabs with rice.

grilled greek patties

Yield: 4 servings

½ pound ground lamb
½ pound ground beef
½ cup fresh bread crumbs
1 teaspoon salt
½ cup finely chopped onion
1 tablespoon dried parsley flakes
¼ teaspoon garlic juice
1 teaspoon crumbled dried mint
1 egg, beaten
¼ cup ouzo
½ cup feta cheese, crumbled

Combine all ingredients except cheese; mix well. Form into 4 patties; chill.

Place patties over hot coals; grill approximately 6 minutes per side, or to desired degree of doneness. Sprinkle with feta cheese 1 minute before removing from grill.

mutton and pork kebabs with mustard sauce

Yield: 6 servings

1 pound mutton cubes
1 pound pork cubes
1 recipe Mustard Sauce
4 slices country-style bacon
1 green pepper
2 medium onions
6 small tomatoes
2 baby eggplants

Combine mutton and pork cubes with Mustard Sauce. Cover; marinate 4 hours.

Remove meat from sauce. Heat sauce; reserve for basting.

Cut bacon into cubes.

Seed green pepper; slice into thick strips.

Peel and quarter onions.

Halve tomatoes.

Slice eggplant into rings.

Thread metal skewers with meat and vegetables, beginning and ending with tomato half. Place kebabs on grill over hot coals; grill 10 to 12 minutes on each side or until desired degree of doneness is reached. Baste frequently with marinade during cooking period.

mustard sauce

Yield: 1¾ cups

2 tablespoons olive oil
¼ cup flour
½ teaspoon seasoned salt
½ teaspoon paprika
1 cup chicken stock
2 tablespoons prepared mustard
½ cup beer

Heat oil in saucepan. Stir in flour and spices; cook until smooth paste forms.

Heat chicken stock; gradually add to flour paste. Stir in mustard. Cook until mixture thickens, stirring constantly. Slowly beat in beer.

Use sauce for basting meats on the grill.

lamb burgers

Yield: 4 servings

1 pound ground lamb
1 teaspoon salt
1 teaspoon monosodium glutamate
¼ cup finely chopped green
    pepper
¼ teaspoon pepper
½ cup soft bread crumbs
1 tablespoon minced onion
4 slices bacon
Mint jelly

Mix together all ingredients except bacon and mint jelly. Form mixture into patties. Wrap each patty in slice of bacon. Grill patties over hot coals 12 minutes or until done. Turn once during cooking period.

Serve burgers with mint jelly.

fresh-catch fried fish

Yield: 4 servings

Oil for frying
2 pounds pan-dressed
    fresh fish
Salt
Lemon-pepper seasoning
2 cups dry pancake mix

fresh-catch fried fish

Place large skillet over open flame or hot coals. Add small amount of oil; heat to just below smoking point.

Sprinkle fish with salt and lemon-pepper seasoning. Dredge in pancake mix. Fry fish about 4 minutes per side. Fish flakes easily with fork when done.

japanese fish kebabs

Yield: 6 servings

1½ to 2 pounds whitefish, cut into
    2-ounce pieces
Salt
14 ounces white miso (soybean
    paste)
1 cup rice wine or sherry
¼ cup sugar

Sprinkle fish with salt. Cover; leave in refrigerator 12 hours.

Mix remaining ingredients. Place fish in mixture; cover. Marinate in refrigerator overnight.

Thread fish on skewers; grill over hot coals about 5 minutes or until fish flakes easily with fork.

eel kebabs

eel kebabs

Yield: 6 servings

2 pounds eel (2 to 3 eels)
1½ cups dry sherry
2 tablespoons honey
¼ cup teriyaki sauce

Skin eels; cut off heads. Remove eel fillets from bone; cut into 1½-inch pieces.

Combine sherry, honey, and teriyaki sauce. Heat to simmer. Pour marinade over eels; let stand 2 hours.

Thread eel on skewers. Place over hot coals; grill 15 to 20 minutes or until fish flakes easily with fork. Baste and turn frequently during cooking period.

halibut with paprika butter

Yield: 4 servings

2 pounds halibut steak
1 cup butter
1 teaspoon paprika
1 teaspoon salt
¼ teaspoon pepper
¼ cup Parmesan cheese

If fish are frozen, thaw before cooking.

Cut fish into serving portions. Place in well-greased hinged wire grills.

Melt butter; combine with paprika, salt, and pepper. Baste fish. Cook fish 4 to 5 inches from grill about 8 minutes. Baste fish; cook remaining side 8 to 10 minutes or until fish flakes easily with fork.

Add Parmesan cheese to remaining sauce. Pour sauce over fish. Serve.

Picture on opposite page: halibut with paprika butter

74

deviled fish steaks

Yield: 4 servings

2 tablespoons hot mustard
1 tablespoon butter, melted
2 tablespoons chili sauce
2 tablespoons horseradish
1 teaspoon salt
4 4- to 6-ounce fish steaks

Combine all ingredients except fish; mix well. Generously butter one side of each steak with sauce. Place on grill over hot coals; grill 5 minutes. Butter raw side of steak; turn steak on grill. Grill 7 to 8 minutes or until fish flakes easily with fork. Serve immediately.

halibut steaks with coffee butter

Yield: 6 servings

1 tablespoon lemon juice   **¼ teaspoon onion powder**
1 tablespoon instant coffee powder **½ teaspoon salt**
¼ cup margarine, melted   **2 pounds fresh halibut steak**

Combine all ingredients except halibut; mix well. Brush liberally on fish. Broil 3 to 4 inches from grill 10 minutes. Turn fish; brush with sauce. Broil 10 minutes or until fish flakes easily with fork.
Brush cooked fish with butter. Serve.

halibut steaks with horseradish

Yield: 6 servings

2 tablespoons lemon juice
1 tablespoon prepared horseradish
¼ cup margarine, melted
2 pounds halibut steak*

Combine lemon juice, horseradish, and margarine; mix well. Brush steaks liberally with sauce. Place on grill 4 inches from hot coals; grill 10 minutes. Brush uncooked side with sauce; turn fish. Broil 10 minutes or until fish flakes easily with fork.
Brush fish with sauce before serving.

* If steaks are frozen, let thaw in refrigerator before grilling.

76

grilled herring with chive butter

Yield: 6 servings

6 drawn herring
½ cup flour
1 recipe Chive Butter (see Index)
Lemon slices
Parsley

Dredge herring in flour. Place in well-greased hinged wire grill. Cook 4 to 5 inches from coals 8 minutes. Turn fish; cook 8 to 10 minutes or until fish flakes easily when tested.

Arrange fish on serving platter; garnish with Chive Butter, lemon slices, and parsley.

grilled herring with chive butter

77

mixed-grill kebabs

Yield: 6 to 8 servings

½ pound sirloin-tip cubes
½ pound pork-loin cubes
¼ pound calves liver, cut into
    strips
6 slices bacon, cut into squares
½ pound squid, cut into small
    pieces
6 jumbo shrimp, peeled, deveined
3 small onions, peeled, cut into
    thick slices
1 red pepper, cut into strips
1 green pepper, cut into strips
6 small tomatoes, cut in half
1 cucumber, sliced into rings
1 cup butter, melted
2 tablespoons minced chives
1 teaspoon salt
¼ teaspoon coarsely ground black
    pepper

Arrange meat, fish, and vegetables in alternate layers on metal skewers, or allow guests to fix their own kebabs.

Combine butter, chives, salt, and pepper; mix well. Baste kebabs with seasoned butter. Place on grill over hot coals; grill about 10 minutes per side or until desired degree of doneness is reached. Baste frequently during cooking period.

ocean perch on the grill

Yield: 4 servings

4 6-ounce perch fillets
½ cup French dressing
Lemon wedges

Place fillets in shallow dish; cover with French dressing. Marinate in refrigerator 4 hours.

Drain fish; place on grill over hot coals. Grill 4 minutes per side or until fish flakes easily with fork. Baste with French dressing while grilling.

Serve perch with lemon wedges.

grilled salmon steaks supreme

Yield: 4 servings

1 tablespoon onion juice
2 tablespoons lemon juice
⅓ cup butter, melted
1 teaspoon salt
¼ teaspoon white pepper
1 tablespoon minced fresh chives
2 tablespoons finely chopped
fresh parsley
4 ¾-inch-thick salmon steaks

Combine all ingredients except salmon; mix well. Brush one side of steaks with sauce; place on grill 4 inches from hot coals. Grill 5 minutes. Turn steaks; baste. Grill 6 minutes or until fish flakes easily with fork.

Heat remaining sauce; serve with cooked steaks.

steamed shrimp

soft-shelled crabs

Yield: 4 servings

¼ cup butter
2 tablespoons fresh-squeezed
    lemon juice
8 soft-shelled crabs, cleaned
1 tablespoon cornstarch
¼ cup water

Melt butter in large cast-iron skillet over hot coals. Add lemon juice; heat to just below boiling. Cook crabs until browned, approximately 6 minutes per side. After crabs are cooked, wrap in aluminum foil; place on edge of grill to keep warm.

Make cornstarch and water paste. Add to pan juices; stir until mixture thickens.

To serve, arrange crabs on serving platter; cover with sauce.

shrimp wrapped in bacon

Yield: 8 servings

4 slices bacon
8 cleaned medium shrimp

Cut bacon strips in half lengthwise. Wrap each shrimp in piece of bacon. Grill over hot coals about 8 minutes or until done.

steamed shrimp

Yield: 6 servings

¼ cup seafood seasoning
4 teaspoons salt
2 cups water
2 cups vinegar
4 pounds medium shrimp

Combine first 4 ingredients in large covered kettle. Place over hot coals; bring to boil. Add shrimp. Cover; steam 20 minutes or until tender. Drain. Serve.

boiled lobster

Yield: 6 servings

1½ gallons water
⅓ cup salt
6 live lobsters (about 1 pound)
Melted butter

Pour water into large kettle; add salt. Cover; bring to boiling point over hot coals. Plunge lobsters headfirst into boiling water. Cover; simmer 20 to 25 minutes, depending on size of lobsters. Drain. Crack claws.

Serve lobster with melted butter.

boiled lobster

chicken and other fowl

west indies chicken halves

Yield: Approximately 1½ cups

¼ cup unsulfured molasses
1 tablespoon prepared mustard
2 tablespoons lemon juice
1 tablespoon Worcestershire sauce
1 can tomato sauce
1 clove garlic, finely chopped
2 tablespoons minced onion
4 chicken halves
Salt
Pepper

Combine molasses, mustard, lemon juice, Worcestershire sauce, tomato sauce, garlic, and onion in small saucepan. Bring to boil; boil 1 minute.

Wash chicken halves; dry thoroughly before grilling. Rub with salt and pepper. Place on center of grill, skin-side-up, 4 to 5 inches above coals. Baste with sauce. Grill 20 minutes. Turn chicken. Baste generously; cook 20 minutes. Turn chicken skin-side-up. Baste; cook 20 minutes or until done.

Note: Baste chicken every 10 minutes to keep meat from drying out.

oregano chicken pieces

oregano chicken pieces

Yield: 4 servings

4 chicken thighs
4 chicken drumsticks
4 chicken breasts
4 chicken wings
½ cup olive oil
¼ cup lemon juice
1½ teaspoons garlic powder
½ teaspoon salt
1 teaspoon oregano
¼ teaspoon pepper

Place all ingredients in large plastic bag. Tie; shake vigorously. Marinate 24 hours in refrigerator.

Remove chicken from marinade; save marinade.

Place chicken on grill over hot coals; grill 15 minutes per side, basting frequently with marinade during cooking period. (For even cooking, place breasts and thighs in center of grill.)

german stuffed chicken breasts

In order to cook the stuffing thoroughly without burning the chicken, this dish should be cooked by the indirect method in a covered cooker to maintain the heat.

Yield: 4 servings

1 cup stewing oysters, raw
4 ounces ground pork
4 chicken livers, finely chopped
1 cup fresh bread crumbs
2 eggs, beaten
1 teaspoon salt
¼ teaspoon pepper
1 small onion, finely chopped
½ cup chopped mushrooms
4 chicken breasts, boned
Butter for basting
3 cups sauerkraut

Combine oysters, pork, livers, bread crumbs, eggs, salt, pepper, onion, and mushrooms; mix well. Fill each breast with equal parts of stuffing mixture. Fasten closed with metal skewers. Place breasts on grill over drip pan. (See Index for indirect cooking method.) Brush with butter. Close lid; cook 30 minutes. Turn chicken breasts; baste with butter.

Pour sauerkraut into heat-proof casserole; place on grill. Cover grill; cook 30 minutes or until internal chicken temperature reads 180°F.

Brush chicken with butter; place on top of heated sauerkraut. Serve immediately.

Picture on next pages: german stuffed chicken breasts

barbecue chicken quarters

Yield: 6 servings

1 8-ounce can tomato sauce
1 tablespoon lemon juice
1 tablespoon Worcestershire sauce
1 teaspoon salt
Dash of hot sauce
2 tablespoons butter, melted
¼ cup grated or finely chopped
**   onion**
6 chicken quarters

Combine all ingredients except chicken; mix well.

Place chicken 4 inches from hot coals. Cook 1½ hours, turning and basting occasionally, or until done. Exact length of time will depend on weight of chicken. To test for doneness, leg should twist easily out of thigh joint.

spicy chicken in foil

Yield: 4 servings

4 chicken quarters
2 tablespoons vegetable oil
1 teaspoon salt
¼ teaspoon pepper
1 onion, finely chopped
1 teaspoon garlic powder
¼ cup finely chopped green
**   chilies**
2 teaspoons dried cilantro
2 fresh medium tomatoes, peeled,
**   chopped**

Wash chicken; pat dry.

Cut 4 10-inch squares of heavy-duty foil. Divide oil among 4 sheets of foil. Grease foil. Place chicken quarter on each foil sheet. Salt and pepper chicken.

Combine remaining ingredients in small bowl. Divide sauce evenly among 4 foil pouches. Fold foil into a neat sealed package. Place packages on grill over hot coals; cook 60 minutes, 30 minutes per side.

Serve chicken from foil packages.

curried chicken–fruit kebabs

A delicious way to serve leftover chicken.

Yield: 4 servings

4 pineapple slices	**2 cups large cubes cooked chicken**
2 apples	**½ cup honey**
2 bananas	**2 teaspoons curry powder**
8 maraschino cherries	**¼ cup lemon juice**

Quarter each pineapple slice.

Core and peel apples; cut into large chunks.

Peel bananas; slice into chunks.

Arrange pineapple, apples, bananas, maraschino cherries, and chicken on skewers.

Combine honey, curry powder, and lemon juice. Baste kebabs. Place kebabs over hot coals; cook about 6 minutes, turning and basting after 3 minutes.

Serve kebabs over bed of rice with chutney.

curried chicken–fruit kebabs

chicken quarters with cucumber sauce

Yield: 4 servings

¼ cup vegetable oil
¼ cup lemon juice
1 cup white wine

1 teaspoon crumbled rosemary
4 chicken quarters

Combine ingredients; place in covered casserole. Marinate in refrigerator 24 hours.

Remove chicken from marinade. Place chicken on grill over hot coals. Grill 1½ hours, turning and basting occasionally, or until done. (To test for doneness, leg should move easily in joint.)

Pour Cucumber Sauce over chicken. Serve.

cucumber sauce

1½ cups sour cream
½ teaspoon garlic powder

1 teaspoon salt
1 cucumber, pureed

Combine ingredients; mix well.

smoked turkey

Smoked meat was once an expensive delicacy because of the equipment needed to smoke meat slowly. Today modern technology has developed a smoker that smokes meat right in your own backyard. If you own a covered grill, you can convert it into a smoker by placing water in the drip pan in the center of the grill and piling hot coals around the drip pan. Cover. Because this is not a true smoker, water and more coals will have to be added about every 4 hours.

Yield: 10 to 12 servings

1 hickory chunk
1 8 to 10 pound turkey

Fill charcoal pan of smoker according to manufacturer's direction. Light charcoals. Allow to get hot (gray) before adding hickory chunk. Fill water pan with hot water; put in place. Position grill. Place turkey on grill; insert meat thermometer. Cover; forget it for 4 hours. (If you peek, you will increase cooking time, owing to heat loss.) After 4 hours add more water and charcoal if needed. Re-cover; let cook 4 more hours. If thermometer does not read 180°F after 8 hours, check each hour thereafter for doneness. Remember to add water and charcoal as needed. If bird was previously frozen, be sure it is completely thawed, or cooking time will be lengthened considerably.

Allow turkey to stand 30 minutes for meat to absorb juices before slicing.

smoked turkey

barbecue turkey roll on rotisserie

Yield: 6 to 8 servings

barbecue sauce

¼ cup diced green pepper
½ cup minced onion
2 tablespoons butter, melted
1 teaspoon garlic powder
1 cup tomato catsup
½ cup chili sauce
¼ cup water
1 teaspoon dry mustard
1 teaspoon prepared horseradish
⅓ cup lemon juice
¼ cup honey
1 tablespoon Worcestershire sauce
1 teaspoon salt
¼ teaspoon pepper

3- to 5-pound turkey roll
Salt
Pepper
½ cup butter, melted

Sauté green pepper and onion in 2 tablespoons butter until lightly browned. Add remaining sauce ingredients. Simmer over low heat 1 hour, stirring occasionally.

Have butcher bone and roll fresh turkey, securing it tightly with string. Rub turkey roll generously with salt and pepper. Insert spit rod through center of turkey roll. Insert skewers firmly in place in roll; screw tightly. Test the balance. Roll must balance on spit so it will rotate smoothly throughout cooking period. Place spit in rotisserie. Brush roast with melted butter.

Arrange hot charcoal briquets at back of firebox. Attach spit with turkey roll. Insert thermometer in center of turkey roll, being sure not to touch spit. Start rotisserie as directed by manufacturer. Cook 2 to 3 hours or until thermometer registers 185°F. Brush with barbecue sauce last 40 minutes of cooking. Remove roast from spit; wrap in foil 30 minutes before slicing to allow roast to absorb juices. Remove string; slice.

orange-glazed duck

orange-glazed duck

Yield: 4 servings

1 fresh 5-pound duckling
Salt
1 cup orange marmalade
2 tablespoons lemon juice

Sprinkle inside cavity of duck with salt. Prepare duck for rotisserie by securing neck skin and closing lower body with metal skewers or clamps. Tie wings and drumsticks to duck's body.* Center duckling on spit. Secure with skewers. Place duck on rotisserie as directed by manufacturer. Place drip pan under duck to catch drippings. Cook by indirect method (see Index) on extremely hot fire approximately 1½ hours or until flesh is no longer pink at leg joints. During last 30 minutes of cooking period, baste with orange marmalade and lemon juice that have been mixed together. Empty drip pan frequently to prevent a fire.

* Some rotisseries come with fowl baskets. If basket is used, you need not secure duck as directed.

vegetables

fresh green beans on the grill

Yield: 6 servings

1 pound fresh green beans
1 teaspoon seasoned salt
6 tablespoons butter
¾ cup water
Chopped parsley
Cherry tomatoes

Wash snap beans; remove ends. Divide beans among 6 12-inch squares aluminum foil. Sprinkle with salt; top with 1 tablespoon butter and 2 tablespoons water per bean package. Wrap beans tightly in foil. Bake on grill 45 minutes or until fork-tender. Turn every 10 minutes during cooking period.

Serve beans garnished with parsley and cherry-tomato halves.

fresh green beans on the grill

baked baby carrots on the grill

Yield: 4 servings

1 pound young baby carrots
4 tablespoons butter
Salt and pepper

Scrub carrots with vegetable brush to remove garden dirt. Leave whole. Place in single layer in 4 pieces of aluminum foil. Top each square with 1 tablespoon butter and salt and pepper to taste. Bake on grill 40 minutes or until tender when tested with point of knife.

brussels sprouts en brochette

Yield: 6 servings

2 10-ounce packages frozen
    brussels sprouts, thawed
1 1-pound can onions, drained
2 medium tomatoes, cut into
    wedges
½ cup French dressing

Arrange vegetables on 6 skewers. Brush lightly with French dressing. Grill 5 inches from coals, 5 minutes per side, basting frequently with dressing.

grilled corn

Yield: 4 servings

8 ears corn
Melted butter

Strip down husks; remove corn silks. Fold husks back over corn. Soak corn in water 1 hour. Drain. Place on grill over hot coals; cook 20 minutes or until tender. Turn ears frequently to ensure even cooking.
Serve corn with melted butter.

corn mexican

Yield: 4 servings

2 tablespoons oil
½ cup chopped green pepper
½ cup chopped onion
¼ cup chopped pimientos
1 16½-ounce can whole-kernel
    corn, drained
½ teaspoon salt
¼ teaspoon pepper

Heat oil in heat-proof casserole with lid. Add green pepper and onion; cook until limp but still crisp. Add remaining ingredients; cover. Heat thoroughly, about 20 minutes. Stir during cooking to prevent scorching.

corn mexican

mushroom kebabs with garlic butter

Yield: 4 servings

24 large mushroom caps
4 cherry tomatoes
½ cup butter
1 teaspoon garlic powder

Place 6 mushrooms on 4 skewers. Top each skewer with cherry tomato.

Melt butter in small saucepan. Stir in garlic powder. Baste kebabs with butter. Place kebabs on grill; cook 10 minutes or until mushrooms are soft. Baste; turn frequently during cooking process.

mushroom kebabs with garlic butter

grilled onion and potato layers

Yield: 4 servings

3 large russet potatoes
1 large Spanish onion
4 tablespoons butter
Salt and pepper to taste

Peel and slice potatoes and onion. Divide evenly among 4 squares aluminum foil. Top each square with 1 tablespoon butter and salt and pepper to taste. Wrap tightly. Place on grill over hot coals; grill 1 hour or until fork-tender.

baked potatoes

The traditional steak-dinner mate.

Yield: 6 servings

6 large baking potatoes
Butter
Sour cream
Chives
Crisp bacon crumbs

Wash potatoes; pierce skins with fork. Wrap each separately in piece of aluminum foil. Bake on grill 1 hour or until tender when pierced with fork.

Serve potatoes in foil pouches with butter, sour cream, chives, and crisp bacon crumbs as garnish.

buttered frozen peas

Yield: 4 servings

1 10-ounce-package frozen peas
3 tablespoons butter
Salt
Pepper

Thaw peas just enough to separate easily with fork. Place peas on large piece of foil; top with butter and salt and pepper to taste. Bring edges of foil into a double fold to form neat package. Fold in sides. Place peas on top of grill over hot coals; grill 15 minutes or until tender.

tangy potatoes and onions

Yield: 4 servings

4 medium onions, sliced into rings
4 medium potatoes, peeled, sliced
**   thin**
¼ cup commercial Caesar's
**   dressing**

Cut 4 pieces aluminum foil about 10-inches square. Place onion and potato on each foil square, alternating layers of onions and potatoes. Pour 1 tablespoon dressing over each serving. Bring up sides of foil. Fold down onto vegetables in tight double folds. Fold ends up in tight double folds. Place on grill over hot coals. Bake 1 hour or until vegetables are fork-tender. Unfold; use foil as serving dish if desired.

cheese-stuffed potatoes

Yield: 4 servings

4 medium baking potatoes
½ cup grated cheddar cheese
Salt
Pepper

Scrub potatoes. Using apple-corer, remove lengthwise piece from center of each potato. Fill each cavity with 2 tablespoons cheese. Plug up ends with potato pieces. Wrap each potato in foil. Bake over hot coals 1 hour or until fork-tender.

rice with mushrooms

A delicious alternative to baked potatoes at your next steak cookout.

Yield: 6 servings

½ cup butter
1 small onion, chopped
1 cup chopped celery
1 cup sliced fresh mushrooms
¼ teaspoon garlic powder
⅓ cup soy sauce
1½ cups cooked rice

Melt butter in cast-iron skillet over hot coals. Add vegetables; cook until heated but still crisp. Add garlic powder, soy sauce, and rice. Move to side of grill; simmer 5 minutes or until hot. Serve immediately.

grilled tomatoes

A delicious way to serve your back-garden rubies.

Yield: 6 servings

6 firm, ripe medium tomatoes
½ cup butter, melted
Dash of Tabasco sauce
½ teaspoon salt
Parsley

Slash an "X" pattern across bottom of each tomato. Remove stem portion from tomato top. Place tomatoes on grill around outside of coals.

Combine butter, Tabasco sauce, and salt. Baste tomatoes frequently while cooking, being sure butter goes into meat of tomato through "X" design. Cook 10 minutes or until tomatoes are heated thoroughly. Lift tomatoes from grill by inserting spatula under tomato to retain its shape.

Serve tomatoes immediately, garnished with parsley.

grilled tomatoes

grilled italian vegetables

Yield: 8 servings

2 zucchini squash
16 cherry tomatoes
8 large mushroom caps
¼ cup butter
¼ cup olive oil

2 garlic cloves, peeled, finely
   minced
1 tablespoon drained, finely
   chopped anchovies
1 teaspoon oregano

Clean vegetables. Cut zucchini into small pieces. Arrange on skewers.

Heat butter and olive oil together 6 inches from grill. Add garlic, anchovies, and oregano. Continue to heat until mixture bubbles and anchovies dissolve. Brush kebabs with mixture. Place on grill 6 inches from hot coals. Cook until vegetables are tender, about 10 minutes, basting and turning frequently. Serve immediately.

grilled italian vegetables

cookout apples

cookout apples

Yield: 4 servings

4 tart apples
2 tablespoons chopped pecans
2 tablespoons raisins
¼ cup butter, melted
¼ cup sugar
½ teaspoon cinnamon
1 can pressurized whipped
**   topping**

Wash and core apples. Scoop out centers to get 1- to 2-inch hole.
Mix nuts and raisins. Fill apples.
Combine butter, sugar, and cinnamon. Pour over apple filling. Place apples in aluminum pan; cover with foil. Bake 4 inches from hot coals 1 hour or until tender.
Serve apples garnished with whipped cream.

10-minute baked apples

Yield: 4 servings

4 medium cooking apples
½ cup sugar
½ teaspoon cinnamon

Place apples on ends of wooden sticks. Hold directly over hot coals; cook 10 minutes, rotating constantly. Remove from fire (do not remove from sticks); peel.

Combine sugar and cinnamon. Roll apples in cinnamon and sugar mixture; eat from stick.

banana delight

A light but fancy dessert to serve at the end of an outdoor feast.

Yield: 4 servings

¼ cup butter
¼ cup sugar
½ teaspoon cinnamon
2 bananas
2 tablespoons rum
¼ cup chopped walnuts

Melt butter in shallow pan over bed of hot coals. (Do this while you enjoy your dinner.)

Mix sugar and cinnamon. Roll banana halves in sugar mixture; cook in melted butter until light brown.

Sprinkle bananas with rum and walnuts just prior to serving.

bananas with honey glaze

Delicious served with homemade ice cream.

Yield: 4 servings

4 bananas
¼ cup lemon juice
2 tablespoons honey
¼ cup chopped toasted almonds

Peel bananas; brush with lemon juice. Place in heat-proof baking dish. Drizzle with honey. Cover with aluminum foil; bake over coals about 25 minutes or until tender.

Remove foil; sprinkle with almonds. Serve immediately.

bananas with honey glaze

105

cherries jubilee with homemade vanilla ice cream

Yield: 6 to 8 servings

**1 recipe Homemade Vanilla Ice
    Cream (see Index)**
¼ cup cherry preserves
1½ tablespoons margarine
2 cups canned pie cherries
½ cup kirsch

Prepare ice cream as directed.

Melt preserves over hot coals on small table grill or burner. Add margarine; stir until melted. Add cherries; heat thoroughly.

In separate pan heat kirsch over coals. Pour heated kirsch over cherries; ignite.

Scoop ice cream into serving dishes. Spoon flaming cherries over ice cream. Serve immediately.

cinnamon graham-cracker sandwiches

Yield: 4 servings

4 large marshmallows
**8 cinnamon graham-cracker
    squares**
**4 .5-ounce milk-chocolate candy
    bars**

Melt marshmallows over hot coals.

Place candy bar on 4 graham-cracker squares. Top with toasted marshmallows and remaining graham-cracker squares. Serve immediately.

Picture on opposite page: cherries jubilee with homemade vanilla ice cream

grilled fruit

Yield: 8 servings

4 bananas
Lemon juice
1 pineapple
4 apples
4 peaches
1 cup granulated sugar
1 teaspoon cinnamon
Butter

Peel bananas; brush with lemon juice.
Peel and core pineapple; slice into rings.
Peel and core apples; slice into rings. Brush with lemon juice.
Peel and halve peaches; remove seed.
Mix sugar and cinnamon thoroughly. Roll prepared fruit in sugar mixture.
Heat butter in large aluminum pan about 6 inches from hot coals. Cook fruit in butter just long enough to soften.

toasted marshmallows

A delicious dessert in your backyard or on a camping trip.

Yield: 4 servings

16 marshmallows
Long branches or forks

Place marshmallow on end of long branch. Hold marshmallow about 3 inches from heat source, rotating branch to ensure even cooking. Cook 1 minute or until marshmallow turns brown. Cool slightly before eating directly from branch.

Picture on opposite page: grilled fruit

homemade vanilla ice cream

Yield: 1½ quarts

½ cup granulated sugar
4 egg yolks
2 cups half-and-half
2 cups whipping cream
2 teaspoons vanilla

Mix sugar and egg yolks in top of double boiler. Pour half-and-half on top of egg-yolk mixture. Cook egg-yolk and half-and-half mixture in double boiler until mixture coats spoon. Cool; strain. Add cream and vanilla. Freeze in conventional ice-cream freezer.

kumquat kebabs

Yield: 6 servings

24 whole maraschino cherries
24 preserved kumquats
1 1-pound can pineapple chunks,
    drained
1 11-ounce can mandarin oranges,
    drained
½ cup honey
1 cup coconut

Layer cherries, kumquats, pineapple, and oranges on 6 skewers. Grill over hot coals 5 minutes. Drizzle with honey; roll in coconut.

go-alongs

camping salad

A delicious salad to serve on your next camping trip.

Yield: 6 servings

8 slices bacon
4 cups salad greens (freshly picked
greens from the wild are
delicious)
2 hard-cooked eggs, chopped
¼ cup salad vinegar
¾ cup corn oil
1 teaspoon salt
Dash of black pepper
½ teaspoon dry mustard

When coals are hot and before you start cooking the main course, fry bacon to a crisp. Drain on brown paper bag; crumble.

Tear greens into bite-size pieces; place in salad bowl. Add bacon pieces and eggs; toss lightly.

Mix vinegar, oil, salt, pepper, and dry mustard in closed container. Shake vigorously until blended. Serve over salad.

grapefruit–fruit salad

Yield: 6 servings

2 pink grapefruits
2 bananas
½ pound blue grapes
1 cup canned pineapple chunks,
   drained
½ cup maraschino cherries
Coconut for garnish

fruit-salad dressing

¾ cup mayonnaise
⅓ cup honey
¼ cup pineapple juice

Peel and section grapefruit. Remove membranes from sections; slice into chunks.

Peel bananas; slice into thin rings.

Halve and seed grapes.

Combine grapefruit, bananas, grapes, pineapple, and cherries; toss gently. Place salad in serving bowl; garnish with coconut.

Prepare dressing by combining mayonnaise, honey, and pineapple juice. Mix well.

mexican potato salad

Yield: 4 servings

4 medium potatoes
1 small onion
½ cup sliced stuffed olives
½ cup parsley
¼ cup olive oil
3 tablespoons red-wine vinegar
½ teaspoon chili powder
½ teaspoon salt
¼ teaspoon pepper
2 hard-cooked eggs, chopped

Scrub potatoes; cook, unpeeled, in boiling, salted water 30 to 40 minutes. Cool; peel; dice. Gently combine potatoes, onion, olives, and parsley.

Mix together olive oil, vinegar, chili powder, salt, and pepper. Add dressing and eggs to salad; toss gently. Chill.

grapefruit–fruit salad

fresh garden salad

fresh garden salad

The perfect match for a barbecue steak.

Yield: 4 servings

2 cucumbers
½ cup white vinegar
½ cup water
1 teaspoon salt
12 cherry tomatoes, sliced into circles

1 green pepper, thinly sliced
1 small sweet onion, peeled, cut into rings
1 tablespoon chopped parsley for garnish

Peel cucumbers; slice crosswise.

Combine vinegar, water, and salt; pour over cucumbers. Marinate at room temperature 2 hours; drain. Add remaining vegetables to cucumbers; toss lightly. Chill before serving.

To serve, arrange on salad plates; garnish with parsley.

114

italian croutons

A pickup for your dinner salad you can make right on your grill.

¾ cup butter
1 loaf cubed French bread
½ cup grated Romano cheese
1 tablespoon oregano
1 tablespoon garlic powder
1 tablespoon basil leaves
1 teaspoon salt
1 teaspoon freshly ground pepper

Melt butter in large skillet over grill. Toss bread cubes with butter, then with cheese and herbs, until well-mixed. Pour bread cubes back into skillet. Fry croutons until golden brown and heated thoroughly. Cool.

Store up to 1 month in an airtight container.

italian croutons

sourdough french bread

A barbecue would not be complete without the traditional loaf of French bread. The next barbecue you host, surprise your guests with homemade sourdough French bread.

Yield: 2 loaves

1 package active dry yeast
1½ cups warm water
1 cup sourdough starter*
1½ cups all-purpose white flour
3 tablespoons granulated sugar
2 teaspoons salt
4½ to 5 cups all-purpose white
**   flour**

Dissolve yeast in warm water. Stir in sourdough starter, blending well. Add the 1½ cups flour; mix well. Let mixture rise overnight or about 12 hours to develop the sponge.

Stire down the sponge. Add sugar and salt; mix well. Add 3 to 3½ cups flour to sponge mixture; work in.

Pour remaining flour onto kneading surface. Pour sponge mixture on top of flour. Knead until all flour has been worked into dough. Continue kneading until folds form in dough (about 10 minutes). Place dough in greased bowl. Grease top of dough. Cover. Let rise in warm place until doubled in bulk. Punch it down.

Turn dough onto lightly floured board. Divide into 2 equal portions. Roll each portion into 15 × 10-inch oblong. Beginning at widest side, roll it up tightly. Pinch edges together. Taper ends by gently rolling dough back and forth. Place loaves on greased baking sheets sprinkled with cornmeal. Cover; let rise in warm place about 1 hour or until doubled in bulk.

With sharp razor make diagonal cuts on top of each loaf. Place loaves in cold oven in which pan of boiling water has been placed. Set oven at 450°F; bake loaves about 35 minutes or until golden crust has formed. Remove bread from oven. Cool on wire rack.

* 1 package active dry yeast
  2 cups warm water
  2 cups all-purpose white flour

Using a stone jar or crock, dissolve the yeast in the warm water. Stir in the flour. Place mixture in warm place for 3 to 4 days or until it is bubbly and smells sour, then refrigerate it.

eddie's sunset french-fried onion rings

An easy vegetable to prepare at home that is extremely expensive when ordered at a restaurant.

Yield: 4 servings

2 large Bermuda onions
½ cup milk
1 cup self-rising flour

Peel onions; cut into medium-thick slices. Place in milk; soak 15 minutes. Dredge in flour. Place in shallow pan; refrigerate 30 minutes before deep-fat frying to golden brown. Drain on paper towel. Serve immediately.

deviled eggs

Yield: 12

6 hard-cooked eggs
¼ cup mayonnaise
1 tablespoon vinegar or pickle juice
1 teaspoon mustard
Salt and pepper to taste
Paprika for garnish

Halve eggs lengthwise; mash yolks. Add mayonnaise, vinegar, mustard, salt, and pepper; mix until smooth. Fill egg-white shells with yolk mixture. Garnish with paprika. Refrigerate.

judy's sweet-and-sour cucumbers

Yield: 8 servings

8 medium-size cucumbers
1 tablespoon salt
1 cup half-and-half
¼ cup apple-cider vinegar
¼ cup granulated sugar

Peel cucumbers. Using potato-peeler, slice cucumbers paper-thin. Sprinkle salt over cucumbers; squeeze with your hands to remove juice from cucumbers. After juice has formed, let cucumbers stand in their own juice at room temperature 1 hour.
Add cream, vinegar, and sugar to cucumbers; mix well. Chill.

pickled eggs

pickled eggs

Yield: 1 dozen

1 quart water
½ cup granulated sugar
1 cup cider vinegar
1 teaspoon salt
1 tablespoon pickling spices
12 eggs

Combine water, sugar, vinegar, salt, and pickling spices. Bring to rolling boil. Cook 10 minutes. Cool to room temperature.

Hard-cook eggs. Peel eggs; place in large container with cover. Add cooled brine; marinate 2 to 7 days, depending on taste preference.

johnnie's sour gherkins with bread

Yield: 4 servings

4 medium-size cucumbers
2 teaspoons salt
½ cup table cream
¼ cup cider vinegar
4 slices white bread
Salt
Pepper

Peel cucumbers. Using potato-peeler, slice cucumbers paper-thin. Sprinkle salt over sliced cucumbers. Squeeze cucumbers with your hands to remove juice. After juice has formed, let cucumbers and juice stand at room temperature 1 hour to wilt cucumbers.

Add cream and vinegar to cucumbers; mix well. Chill before serving.

Serve cucumbers over bread slices. Salt and pepper to taste.

bread-and-butter pickles

If you are lucky enough to own a food processor, you can slice these pickles in 15 minutes.

Yield: 12 pints

2½ gallons cucumbers, unpeeled,
sliced paper-thin
4 large Spanish onions, peeled,
sliced paper-thin
3 large sweet green peppers,
clean, sliced into
paper-thin strips

¼ cup pickling salt*
4 cups cider vinegar
4 cups granulated sugar
2 tablespoons mustard seed
1½ teaspoons turmeric
½ teaspoon whole cloves

Layer cucumbers, onions, green peppers, and pickling salt in 6-gallon container. Cover with crushed ice; let stand 4 hours. Drain; rinse in ice-cold water.

Combine vinegar, sugar, mustard seed, turmeric, and cloves to form pickling brine. Stir to dissolve sugar. Bring pickling brine to boil. Add drained vegetables; again bring mixture to boil. Remove from heat immediately. Pack vegetables into sterilized jars. Cover with pickling brine to ½ inch from jar rim. Seal jars; process in boiling-water bath 15 minutes.

* Do not use table salt; it will make your pickling brine cloudy.

orange cups

Yield: 8 servings

4 eating oranges
2 tablespoons wild-flower honey
½ cup whole cranberry sauce

Cut oranges in half. Carefully remove insides, being careful to keep skins intact. Cut orange meat into small pieces, removing skin and seeds. Drizzle honey over orange pieces; toss gently. Fill orange halves with orange chunks; garnish with cranberry sauce.

baklava

A delicious picnic dessert that improves with age and, more important, does not require refrigeration.

Yield: 24 servings
honey syrup

1 small lemon   **1 piece stick cinnamon**
1 cup sugar   **4 whole cloves**
1 cup water   **1 cup natural honey**

Remove zest from lemon. Squeeze 1½ teaspoons lemon juice from lemon; set aside. Combine lemon zest, sugar, water, cinnamon stick, and cloves in heavy saucepan. Bring to boil. Lower heat; continue cooking without stirring 25 minutes (230°F on candy thermometer). Stir in honey. Remove spices. Add lemon juice. Stir; allow to cool.

cake

½ pound butter, melted   **½ cup sugar**
1 pound phyllo sheets   **1½ teaspoons cinnamon**
1 pound walnuts, finely chopped

Brush 13 × 9 × 2-inch baking dish with some of melted butter.
Fold phyllo sheet in half; place in dish. Brush with butter. Top with another folded phyllo sheet; brush with butter.
Combine nuts, sugar, and cinnamon in small bowl; mix well. Top phyllo with ½ cup sugar mixture. Top with 2 more folded phyllo sheets, brushing each with butter. Continue process until 2 phyllo sheets remain. Fold, butter, and layer to form top crust. With razor blade cut through top dough layer to make 24 servings. Bake at 325°F 50 minutes. Remove from oven and, with sharp knife, cut through all layers of pastry. Pour cooled syrup over pastry; cool. Cover; let stand at least 24 hours.

double-chocolate cake

Yield: 24 servings

2 cups granulated sugar	½ cup shortening
2 cups all-purpose white flour	1 cup hot water
¼ cup cocoa	½ cup sour milk
½ teaspoon salt	2 eggs, beaten
1 teaspoon soda	1 teaspoon vanilla

Combine sugar, flour, cocoa, salt, and soda; set aside.

Bring shortening and water to boil. Remove from heat; stir in dry ingredients. Add milk, eggs, and vanilla; mix thoroughly. Pour cake batter into greased 9 × 13-inch pan. Bake at 375°F 25 minutes or until toothpick inserted into center comes out clean. Remove cake from oven; frost immediately.

chocolate–walnut frosting

⅓ cup half-and-half	1 pound powdered sugar
½ cup butter	1 teaspoon vanilla
⅓ cup cocoa	½ cup English walnuts, chopped

Combine half-and-half, butter, and cocoa in saucepan; bring to boil. Add powdered sugar and vanilla; beat until well-blended. Stir in walnuts. Spread on cake while frosting and cake are still warm.

carolyn's banana cheesecake

Yield: 8 servings

1¼ cups graham-cracker crumbs	1 15-ounce can condensed milk
¼ cup granulated sugar	⅓ cup lemon juice
⅓ cup butter, melted	2 bananas
1 8-ounce package cream cheese, softened	1 cup whipped cream

Mix crumbs, sugar, and butter in 9-inch pie pan until crumbs are well-moistened. Press mixture evenly on bottom and sides of pan. Bake 8 minutes at 400°F.

Beat cream cheese until fluffy. Gradually add milk; beat until well-blended. Add lemon juice; blend well.

Mash 1 banana; blend into cream-cheese mixture.

Slice remaining banana over crust. Pour filling on top of bananas. Chill thoroughly.

Serve topped with whipped cream.

rainbow cake

An attractive centerpiece for a backyard barbecue.

Yield: 12 servings

frosting

5 tablespoons flour
1 cup milk
1 cup margarine
1 cup granulated sugar
1 teaspoon vanilla

Blend flour with ¼ cup milk to form smooth paste. Add remaining milk to paste; cook until stiff paste forms. Cool until cold.

Cream margarine and sugar. Add to paste; blend. Add vanilla; beat until frosting takes on appearance of whipped cream.

2 9-inch white-cake layers	1 to 2 drops yellow food coloring
1½ cups shredded coconut	1 to 2 drops green food coloring
1 to 2 drops red food coloring	3 teaspoons milk

Frost and fill top and sides of cake layers.

Divide coconut evenly among 3 jars. Mix each food coloring with 1 teaspoon milk; pour 1 color in each of 3 jars of coconut. Cover jars; shake until coconut is evenly tinted. Combine tinted coconut. Cover top and sides of frosted cake.

fruit ice

A unique and refreshing way to decorate the drinks at your next barbecue.

Yield: 18 ice cubes

Assorted berries in season
Whole fruit in season

Wash and remove stems from berries.

Wash whole fruit; cut into chunks that will fit ice-tray cubicles.

Distribute fruit among ice cubicles. Fill with water. Freeze until firm. Use 1 fruit cube per glass.

fruit ice

mulled cider

A delicious treat to serve parents of Halloween trick and treater's.

Yield: 1 gallon

1 gallon fresh-pressed apple cider
2 oranges, sliced, seeded
2 lemons, sliced, seeded
1½ sticks cinnamon
6 whole cloves

Combine all ingredients in large stock pot with lid. Place over hot coals about 6 inches from coals. Heat at least 1½ hours before serving.

mulled cider

haberman's hot butterscotch milk

A delicious breakfast drink for your next campout.

Yield: 8 servings

**1 6-ounce package butterscotch
    chips
½ gallon whole milk
1 can pressurized whipped cream**

Soften butterscotch chips over hot coals. Whip with wire whisk to liquify.
Heat milk over coals. Add heated milk slowly to melted chips, whipping with whisk while adding milk.
Pour into serving glasses; garnish with whipped cream.

tasty-aide

A tart version of the sweetened flavored drinks. Using less sugar, this drink will quench your thirst and save money.

**1 .24-ounce package unsweetened
    drink mix
½ cup sugar
1½ quarts water**

Pour drink mix and sugar into 2-quart pitcher. Add water; mix well. Chill before serving.

index